THE ORIGINS OF HUMAN BEHAVIOUR

by
Bernard Rourke

Strategic Book Publishing and Rights Co.

Strategic Book Publishing and Rights Co.
12620 FM 1960, Suite A4-507
Houston TX 77065
www.sbpra.com

ISBN: 978-1-61897-679-6

Table of Contents

Foreword

The medical profession has made such progress during the last century that we are now healthier and live longer. They have been pro-active in educating the public on health matters and raising awareness of the steps that can be taken to remain healthy. Television has been a medium they have used well. We can be satisfied that the physical well-being of *Homo sapiens* is in good hands.

The same cannot be said for the professionals in the *mental* health community. There has been a distinct lack of effort to raise public awareness of mental health issues, even allowing for the fact that explaining the mind and human behaviour is more problematic than describing body organs. Critics could claim that the public knows as little about human behaviour and mental disorders today as it did when Queen Victoria died.

Is this ignorance because the public does not wish to understand such matters? Are mental health disorders still a taboo subject or, even worse, do the professionals feel they have nothing worthwhile to tell us?

The outcome is that the public receives no encouragement, incentive, direction, or reading material to decide whether or not they *are* interested in learning more about the workings of the mind and associated behaviour.

This book has been written to provide comments, opinions, and theories in plain English on this subject. It covers aspects of human behaviour, the mind and mental health disorders. In short, it sets out to find the **origins of human behaviour.** It is written in the hope that ordinary people will discover whether or not they are interested in the subject. If they are, they will require more readable books and watchable television programmes, and the professionals will have to be raising public awareness of the current state of mental health. At the moment, we have no reason to feel confident that our mental health is "in good hands."

The mental health professionals will be the first to point out that I am not a trained psychologist or psychiatrist. (If I were, would I be writing this book in plain English?)

I am confident I have a message to relay to those wishing to hear it, and let the professionals mock and criticise if they so wish.

At one stage, I did wonder whether I was trying to be too clever (or stupid), so I contacted a practising psychiatrist to ask for her professional opinion as to the "believability" of some of my conclusions. She told me she found them "interesting."

"I never came across such ideas when I was studying but, if you ever write a book, I will be one of the first to buy a copy."

Introduction

Many psychologists and psychiatrists would have us believe that, because our minds are empty vessels at birth, it is life's experiences filling them with emotions and memories that serve as the foundation of all we become as human beings. They claim **external factors** strongly influence the development of our character and behaviour, so it was inevitable and convenient for them to identify traumatic experiences as the **main cause** of many mental health illnesses and behavioural problems.

I consider this to be a blinkered approach. I believe our minds are far from "empty" at birth. In fact, I am convinced that what we inherit serves as the cornerstone of who we are and the person we become. Life's experiences may impact on our development, but our ability to handle them will be strongly influenced by what I will term our *genetic core.*

So, one side claims that life's experiences are the major factor moulding us (*environmentalism*), and the other that genetic influences provide the core of who we are (**heredity**). This is known as the **Nature versus Nurture** argument.

Whichever side is right, it has a great deal to answer for. *Homo sapiens* have shown themselves to be the cruellest, most self-centred and mentally fragile species on earth. How could we, the so-called pride of evolution, contain so many flaws?

Fortunately, we are a relatively young species and still evolving. Medical advances have certainly helped our physical development. Perhaps now is the time to take steps to reassure ourselves that similar progress can be made in mental health.

To continue claiming environmental factors to be the main cause of criminal behaviour is misleading. More consideration should be given to raising the level of public interest and awareness of other influential factors.

The media regularly offer information on new techniques and improved survival rates in important physical diseases. The mental health professionals offer no such information. The public does not even know whether there are any. If there are major disagreements within the mental health profession, the public should be made aware of them, especially if they may be inhibiting essential progress. It would be better for the public who, at the moment, are in mental health limbo land.

The attitude of the professionals should be more along the lines of *"Awareness and prevention can be better than a cure."*

We don't understand human behaviour. We are touched by the humanity of some people and weep at the inhumanity of others. Which factors direct us to behave as we do? Surely we deserve better explanations than the proverbial offerings of *"bad homes and bad parents."*

The aim of this book is not to criticise psychologists and psychiatrists. It is to offer ideas and explanations to the public as to which factors are, or could be, decisive in our behavioural development. It provides some information on mental and behavioural matters with the aim of encouraging the public to want to learn more about the subject. Finally, it is to ask the professionals to consider ways in which they could promote greater awareness of mental health issues. The image of mental illness desperately needs to be improved and updated.

If there is to be significant mental development during our evolutionary process, there is a need for better understanding (by all of us) of the human mind and its impact on behaviour. We are still in the age where descriptive words like *nutters* and *crackers* and *loony bins* are used. We have plenty of empathy for people suffering from cancer or broken bones, but still want to tell people who are severely depressed to "snap out of it."

You may be wondering what placed this bee under my bonnet—what got me so worked up about people, their character, and behaviour?

My fascination started in my teens because of my four brothers (I was the next to youngest). We were such different individuals, I mean *really* different, in so many ways, I could not believe we came from the same parents, and frequently thought the other four must have been adopted. *"How could five sons from a stable home be so dramatically different?"* I kept asking myself.

As I got older and became more aware of the world we live in, I realised my family was merely a microcosm of humanity, because behaviour generally is complicated, multi-faceted, and very confusing. My personal interest then developed into a search for answers about human behaviour in general. We all wonder how some people can be so selfless, while the rest of us are utterly selfish.

Can we really blame life's experiences for our individual blessings and failings, or is there much more to it than that?

What makes us behave as we do? Which factors contribute to making us the person we become? Could we have more input into our own development or do we all just *"evolve" in our own little bubble?*

These are difficult questions admittedly, but the medical profession's interest in helping us understand our body made me somewhat resentful of what I considered to be inertia in the "mental" health profession.

For decades, we have feasted on brilliant television programmes explaining animal behaviour, and there are constant medical programmes explaining the causes and new treatment of physical ailments. The mind and its ailments, or series on human behaviour, have been glaringly absent from our screens. Is there some kind of reluctance to discuss the subject openly? If so, why? There must be a market for it.

Enormous amounts of research have been carried out on the subject, and there are innumerable opinions floating about, so it cannot be that they have nothing to say. Unfortunately for those of us who would like to read such information, publication of this kind of research faces two major problems.

Firstly, professionals experience difficulty in producing research material that can be proven and validated to the high standards required by the scientific community. As a consequence, too much research concludes with, *"The results are inconclusive and further research is needed."*

Secondly, the material they do publish is written in jargon language, way beyond the ordinary reader's grasp. You know what I mean—after every two words, your hand reaches for the dictionary. Eventually, frustration and boredom set in.

The outcome of all this is that ordinary, interested people are without encouragement, direction, or accessible reading material.

As a layman, I am not encumbered by restrictions. I am able to express my opinions and conclusions without fearing professional criticism. Quite the opposite, I would welcome it.

My qualifications for writing this book are **Certificates** for decades of observation and reading, **Diplomas** for wanting to understand and learn about human behaviour, and **Satisfaction** from believing I have something worth saying. I cannot claim to be right, but if others claim my conclusions are wrong, I would expect them to provide better, more believable explanations.

Perhaps the real claim that this book will be worth reading is it is a **starting point** for the interested, but uninformed, reader. It questions whether we should blame the world we live in for all our faults or if we are more capable than we think of influencing who we are and how we behave.

After all, the society we live in does its best to turn us into good children, good teenagers, good adults, good parents, and good citizens. As it goes wrong for so many of us, does that mean society failed us, or did we contribute to our own successes and failures?

You may agree with some or all of my findings, or you may not. But at least you will be exposed to ideas, theories, and opinions to consider and reject. This is a beginning.

Disagreeing with a point of view can be just as valuable as agreeing with it. It proves you are developing your own. You may well go on to search the Internet to expand your knowledge.

Human behaviour is controlled and directed by the brain. We all know how complex that is. Offering finite explanations on its workings is more than difficult. Perhaps that is why the scientific community appears to be frightened of exposing themselves to the public. Their world is closed to the rest of us by a wall of specialist terminology. It is either that, or they also think we are not interested in learning more about ourselves. If this is so, then we must accept some blame.

Their public silence could almost be considered an admission that mental illness should **not** be spoken about, or even worse, they have nothing worth saying.

The only time I hear any of their opinions on behaviour is when they are claiming in court that some criminals acted as they did because they came from a broken home, lived in a slum area, or some other negative influences. I never hear them saying that social workers, nurses, and teachers do what they do because they came from a broken home in a slum area, as many of them do!

It can't be because they think we are incapable of understanding. Why? Because if we are incapable of understanding **before** we become mentally ill, what chance would there be of understanding **after** we are ill and receiving treatment? I wish they would just come out and say what they believe, so there can be some kind of public debate on the subject. Today, the best medium would be television.

I realised my journey for answers had started when watching television programmes on animal behaviour. They seemed to be suggesting paths for me to follow, ideas worthy of investigation.

Decades later, I eventually reached the point where my searching had resolved a large number of the issues that had long baffled me. In a satisfying way, I feel closer to my brothers, even though now I am the only one still alive. It was a journey I was glad I had undertaken.

It then occurred to me that there must be many as mystified as I by the behaviour of themselves and others, who might appreciate having some readable material on the subject. After all, you won't know whether you are interested unless you can read something about it first. This is your chance.

The beauty of this book is that I am not trying to persuade you that I am a great scientist with brilliant conclusions and ideas. I chose the title *The Origins of Human Behaviour,* not because I consider myself to be another Charles Darwin, but because that was what I set out to find. Over the years, I have had wonderful discussions (and arguments) around the dinner table with family and friends. I hope you will, too. You might move on to seek more information before making up your own mind on the various issues and hopefully develop better theories.

If you disagree—brilliant! If the scientific community dismisses my ideas—excellent, so long as their criticism is followed by better explanations. Theories cannot be dismissed as incorrect unless they are replaced by theories that are more believable. And at that point, we would finally have a public debate on human behaviour and the workings of the mind. **Success!**

I want discussions on behaviour to be informative, thought provoking, interesting, believable and available for all who express an interest in learning about it. But the process will not come about unless the public decides they will benefit from exposure to ideas on human behaviour, and want more information and material to be made available to them. Only the general public calling for a better understanding of the mind, mental illness, and related matters will prompt the professionals to adopt a more pro-active approach, along the lines taken by the medical profession.

Such a development will also promote a greater awareness and sympathy for people with mental disorders.

Although my original goal was to understand more about *human* behaviour, I soon accepted that my journey must begin by looking at other species in the animal kingdom.

We, *Homo sapiens*, are the latest members of that kingdom. If the laws of evolution are to be believed, much of what existed before carries on into later species. Much of what we possess as a species has evolved, been tested and improved over millions of years by countless successful species. What was successful survived, and all that success was then carried forward into later species.

We are the latest recipient of the hundreds of millions of years of trial and error, chance, and accidents and, most of all, evolutionary development. Our brains are the best, our dexterity the greatest, our mental potential is unbelievable, and our behaviour is the most infuriatingly complex of all the animals on earth.

If, while reading this book, you say, *"I never thought of it that way,"* or you should feel it was not a mistake to start reading it, I shall be more than satisfied.

Part 1 looks at interesting aspects of animal behaviour and considers their origin and effectiveness (because what works for them might be working for us).

Part 2 examines interesting behavioural traits in humans and tries to ascertain whether they are the result of natural (**inherited**) factors or have been mainly developed and nurtured by life's experiences since birth (**environmental**).

Part 3 discusses certain external issues, embraced by millions of people worldwide, which influence their thinking and behaviour.

Part 4 discusses the possible benefits for us of having a greater understanding of the **origins of behaviour.**

Enjoy the journey.

PART ONE – ANIMAL BEHAVIOUR

A look at instinctive behaviour and other inherited features in the non-human animal kingdom to ascertain whether they offer any clues for a realistic insight into human behaviour

An Itsy-Bitsy Spider

Many years ago, I was watching a spider making its web between the ceiling and door of an outside toilet at home. I remember it so clearly. Industrious little thing it was, constructing one of those dartboard webs. So clever. Skilful. A work of art. A silky piece of architecture. Even though I was only in my early teens, I could appreciate the artistry involved, and it was not long before I was smiling as I imagined the mother spider lining up all her baby spiders on a branch to instruct them in the technique and importance of making such a web:

"If you make it properly and place it in a good location, you will catch plenty of insects and have a long and interesting life. A poorly made web will catch very little, and you will starve. Do you understand? Well, watch me once more, and then go off and practise until you get it perfect."

That was a ridiculous idea and even I guessed it didn't happen. Then it dawned on me that my spider was not just clever and skilful, it must be brilliant! It had to be, constructing this beautifully, efficient, dartboard web without being taught how to do it. Incredible!

I asked my mother about it and she casually attributed it to *"instinct,"* explaining that all animals have instinctive abilities that enable them to do things without being taught—things that help them to "survive in their harsh world."

I was impressed and went to the dictionary immediately to learn a little more about *"instinct."* I discovered such words as *"innate"* and *"inborn abilities."* Certain animal behaviour was simply described as *"instinctive"* (unthinking).

When I watched nature programmes on TV, they regularly referred to *instinct* and *instinctive behaviour* as if everyone understood exactly what that meant:

"Salmon travel thousands of miles to return to their river of origin to spawn. This amazing behaviour is driven by instinct."

"The newly hatched turtles push their way up through the sand and automatically head for the safety of the sea. This is instinctive behaviour."

After mentioning the *"i"* word, the commentator would always move on as if nothing else needed to be added. *Instinct.* Ah, yes. Everyone knows what that is. No explanation needed.

I realised that others could not be as massively impressed as I was. Well, perhaps they were impressed, but not as curious about it. Certain animal behaviour may have been incredible, but it was soon obvious to me that *instinct* was being used as a convenient all-inclusive word for what was considered as merely unthinking, involuntary, automatic, knee jerk, reflex behaviour, like your leg jerking forward after a tap below the knee—an instinctive response that did not need thinking about. No big deal.

I cannot recall anyone in the nature programmes ever trying to explain what instinct was apart from *"something they are born with."*

The dictionary definitions irritated me for a long time. Eventually, I realised that a better word for "innate" and "inborn" was *"inherited"* (although this word was not used in any of the dictionaries I first consulted). It made sense to me. They were born with certain abilities, which had been passed on to them at birth, which they had "inherited." So, why not say it!

One definition of "inherit" is *"to possess (a characteristic) through genetic transmission."* To me, that seemed to apply perfectly to instinct. Human beings "inherit" diseases, but animals never "inherited" instincts, yet both are inborn and genetically transmitted.

The point I am making is that, quite early on, I felt that animal "instinct" was almost being downgraded. These majestic and magical gifts were all being dismissed with a single word. If it had been human behaviour, everyone would have been ecstatic but, because it involved insects or other animal life, it was no big deal.

As soon as I started thinking of "instinctive behaviour" as being *"inherited behaviour"* it made more sense to me. My spider had been born with the ability to construct a web that would catch food for it. No instruction or training was needed. Its tiny brain contained *at birth* all the knowledge and skill it needed to help it to survive. It was a means of assisting its survival.

This was amazing. The animal kingdom had evolved or been given (depending on your upbringing) innate, inborn, inherited, instinctive abilities (call them what you will) to help them survive. That realisation changed the way I have looked at my family, others, and myself for over sixty years. It excited me.

Then years later, I was really blown away when, in a TV nature programme, I first heard about the *Monarch* butterfly in North America. Each year, this species undertakes a **five month** migration of about three thousand miles from the Great Lakes to Mexico and back (using the same stop-over points annually), during which they mate and produce and eventually die along the way.

Each generation on this journey lives for only four to five weeks yet, no matter at which point during the *five-month* migration a Monarch butterfly is born, it not only inherits the information it needs to continue the next phase of its journey, but it inherits all the information required to pass on details of the *whole journey* to the next generation—*even though none of them would live long enough to travel through those parts of the journey.*

Information passed on covers route, resting places, and specific type of leaves on which to lay the eggs—the full itinerary!

I felt that to dismiss this feat merely as "instinctive" (which happened when I first saw it on television) was criminal. At the time, I thought it was one of the wonders of the world! It amazed me that a butterfly (albeit a biggish one) has the urge and the guts to undertake the journey, inherits the knowledge of the whole route (even regular rest-over points), and later passes on the same gift of knowledge to its next generation. Yet because it was a mere insect, this feat, this outstanding achievement, was explained, justified, and dismissed in a word—*Instinct.*

I can still recall how incensed I was that I had been left hanging in the air at the end of the programme. There I was, mouth open at the wonder of everything that contributed to such a journey, with so many questions about it that I wanted answered, and it had ended. To me, the programme had only just begun! Yet a single word had answered and dismissed any potential questions about the incredible journey of the Monarch butterfly. It was like having "The End" shown in the cinema when you felt you were just getting into a good story.

It was at that point that I began to think seriously about instinct in the animal kingdom and its possible significance for humans. We belong to that kingdom. We are on the same tree of life. If the infinitesimal brains of a spider and butterfly could inherit such gifts of knowledge, where did that leave Man? Our brains are gargantuan by comparison. What gifts could our species inherit?

You will note I have been using such words as *abilities, knowledge, and gifts* as being inherited. To me, it is inconceivable that the Monarch butterfly travels long journeys *without thinking* about what it is doing, or that spiders construct and repair their webs *"in a dream-like state."* Yet people seem to dismiss it as *unthinkingly* instinctive, as if all animals are robotic zombies.

Many people consider instinct to be an "automatic pilot" thing with no thought involved. Just do it. Instinct dictates how a particular species of bird builds an intricate hanging nest, so when it is time to construct one (without any previous instruction or experience), the bird doesn't even have to press an instinct button. It just builds one like an automaton. "Unthinking behaviour." Poppycock!

We are told that some female spiders are likely to eat the smaller male after mating. Whichever part of the mating procedure is considered "instinctive," no-one will convince me that the male spider is not thinking himself silly as to how he is going to get out of there without being eaten before or after mating. If it was an unthinking, instinctive urge leading him to mate with a bigger spider-eating female, he certainly wasn't going through an unthinking process as he worked out how to escape her clutches after the desperate deed was done. This leads me to another essential conclusion during my early journey.

A spider may have inherited the ability to build a web, but it needs a thought process and decision-making ability to determine where to build it and how to repair it. They must have active minds to help them survive on their own during their lifetime. Nature has endowed them with the gifts of ability and knowledge to help them survive. They inherit knowledge and abilities. It is the same knowledge retained in the memory bank of its parents, to be called upon and passed on as and when needed.

That was when I concluded that a more accurate description of *instinct* would be ***inherited memories!***

Knowledge is not a physical entity. It is information stored in the brain that is gifted to future generations at the time of conception. We have come to call these inherited memories *"instinct"* because they resulted in a behaviour passed down in the species. A clearer definition of instinct would therefore be ***"genetically transmitted knowledge that leads to behaviour common to a particular species."***

We have been told that animals can be trained to give a conditioned response to certain stimuli. A famous example was *Pavlov* and his dogs. In his experiments, he repeatedly exposed dogs to a certain stimulus (e.g., ringing a bell) and their reward would be food. The dogs eventually became so conditioned with this treatment that when a bell rang, they began to salivate in anticipation of a reward. I remember being told about this in school. Apparently, the world was agog at this achievement in 1901. The implication was that it was an immediate, unthinking, *conditioned*, instinctive response to the bell without any input by the individual dog. I am not so sure.

If I were placed in a room with doors in it and each time a bell was rung, a beautiful, semi-clad maiden opened one of them and beckoned me invitingly, I know that, no matter how backward I was when younger, it would not have taken me long to salivate *with anticipation* at the ringing of the bell.

Conditioned response maybe, but never in this world would it have been an "unthinking response." I would have been rushing to the door shouting "Hallelujah! Here I come."

I do not have the qualifications, nor would I wish, to criticise a person like *Pavlov* who, after all, received a Nobel Prize (but not for the dogs experiments), but I do feel that his research contributed to the *"unthinking, instinctive, conditioned behaviour in animals"* mentality.

Having convinced myself of the transfer of memories (knowledge) at birth, I felt it opened all possibilities for the human brain. But a closer inspection of the type of memories being gifted was necessary. Web building was distinctly different from inheriting route maps for a five-month butterfly migration or the salmon's desperate need to cross the oceans to return to a specific river to spawn.

Instinct is rampant in the animal kingdom. I needed to learn about other types of memories in the animal kingdom that *might* tell us more about ourselves.

I kept thinking, *"If the tiny brains of insects could do so much for them, what could our minds do for us?* My mind was doing cartwheels.

What exactly is *Instinct?*

Before we decide whether or not *Homo sapiens* inherit any form of instinct, we need to have a clearer understanding of its scope. For this we must stay with the animal kingdom.

We can accept that "Instinct leads to behaviour that is inherited, not learned," but here are other questions that need explaining.

How influential is instinct on behaviour?

Is "instinctive behaviour" the same as **unthinking behaviour?**

What different types of instinct are there?

Is it always 100 percent implanted in each member of the species or can it be less influential in some individuals?

Can instinctive behaviour change?

Can instincts evolve?

Answers to such questions are important before we consider whether it is possible for humans to inherit such "robotic" controls on our behaviour.

How influential is instinct on animal behaviour?

Instinctive behaviour is so influential that it still amazes and baffles scientists—so much so that, in my opinion, they almost use the term *instinct* to describe "any animal activity they cannot explain." Furthermore, they use it and associated words in such a definitive way to imply that no further explanation is necessary. They do this, not because they know you understand how instinct works, **but because they don't**. It is as if they don't want to believe that knowledge and skills can be genetically transferred from one generation to another in species more primitive than our own, but they cannot avoid acknowledging they exist as an impressive phenomenon in the animal kingdom.

Is "instinctive" behaviour the same as "unthinking" behaviour?

I think the scientists would like us to believe this because then it does not require explaining. The doctor taps under our knee and the lower leg jerks forward. That is a reflex action. This is a good example of physical *unthinking behaviour*. We all know that. But the scientists have tried to convince us that magical animal instinctive behaviour involving knowledge and skills is akin to the **physical** act of a human knee-jerk. Don't believe them.

Constructing webs, building nests, and undertaking migrations are physical activities that must require knowledge, concentration, decision-making, and adapting to changing circumstances. They are not tasks being completed in an immediate, zombie-like state. To say insects or animals live their lives without having to think insults the species. I still cannot believe that any reputable scientist could confidently support such a theory today.

The view that humans do not inherit instincts is partly based on the belief that we do not **need** them and we are not capable of carrying out *"unthinking acts in a zombie-like fashion."* I have not heard it said that we do not have instincts because we **cannot** have them.

How many categories of instinct exist?

We know that the *Monarch* butterfly has at least four types of instinctive behaviour:

(1) The *ability* to fly is a skill that some might claim falls into the *unthinking* category

(2) The innate *urge* to migrate at a given time of the year.

(3) Possession of the knowledge needed for the whole journey.

(4) The ability to pass on the knowledge to the next generation.

The first is almost "robotic"; the second is an inner need; the third is its inheritance package; and the fourth is an amazing genetic transfer of information. These are four different aspects of inherited gifts that strongly influence one insect's behaviour, and all are essential for that species.

Salmon also have an inner driving force that makes them return to their place of origin when it is time to mate and spawn, and they also inherit the ability to find their way there from thousands of miles away.

Such gifts are impossible to explain apart from saying they are *instinctual*. Humans who try to explain it are forced to explain it as if humans were carrying out the tasks. A basic question is, "Did the species survive because of these instincts, or did the instincts evolve when the species survived?" I think the latter.

My mother's comment that *"Instinct enables them to survive in a harsh world"* is a commonly held view. The spider's ability to survive because it knows how to build a web is a good example. But instinct can also include less important behavioural patterns.

We have seen on TV the footage of exotic male birds performing specific plumage displays to persuade a female to choose them as mates. All the males of the species perform similar routines (with varying success). This is instinctive mating behaviour (we are told). They all know the object of the game and are putting heart and soul into what they were doing. Obviously, this behaviour pattern evolved in the species. Presumably, from all the early different means of attracting the females, exotic plumage displays proved to be the most stimulating, and this successful process, in time, became instinctive for the males. No doubt it also led to increased male plumage growing in the species as the female kept selecting the best examples for mates. Over time, this behaviour became an *evolved* instinctive mating ritual of the species. Let's face it, male and female animals of any species can recognise each other. They need mating to satisfy a biological need, and mating rituals evolve by choice. Strange how the mating is biological, yet we classify the selection process as instinctive.

Scientists have long argued over the possibility of humans inheriting *instincts*. When the subject first became popular, one "scientist" claimed that Man inherited up to four thousand. Over the decades, this was gradually whittled down until Freud claimed the only instinct in Man's make-up was the "*id*." (This is the so-called primitive part of our brain, determined to pursue selfish things such as eating, copulation, and self-survival).

I came across a declaration by some scientist in which he laid down a number of criteria for determining instinctive behaviour in animals. These were:

- *automatic*
- *irresistible*
- *occur at some point in development*
- *be triggered by some event in the environment*

- *occur in every member of the species*
- *be unmodifiable*
- *govern behaviour for which the organism needs no training (although experience may lead to modified behaviour)*
  **(The absence of one or more of these criteria indicates that
  the behaviour is not fully instinctual.)**

Such criteria seemed to be describing a robot's behaviour and helped to reinforce the view that, apart from things such as physical features and illnesses, humans could not possibly have genetic inheritance of so-called *instincts* or *memories.*

On the other hand, if you delete *"occur in every member of the species,"*, the remaining criteria could be attributable to all of us at some stage in our lives. So, now we have other aspects of genetic inheritance to think about:

- *"Does an acknowledged instinct in a species occur in every member?"*
- *"When it is present, does it always have the **same** controlling influence on the resulting behaviour?"*

Don't start thinking I am going all scientific and switch off. I am excited about such ideas because they give us more ammunition for shooting down the theories that instinctive behaviour is unthinkingly robotic and inflexible. Such matters may become important where humans are concerned.

If inherited memories (skills, etc.) vary in effectiveness (i.e., have little or no influence on some animal's behaviour within the species), then instinct is not a finite item within that species.

Another point is that, although all instincts *are* genetically transferred, it is not necessarily true that all *genetically transferred characteristics are **instincts**.* I will discuss this in more detail in a later chapter.

Since we are led to believe that instinct has been ever-present in the animal kingdom from the most primitive species onwards, we must seriously consider whether this phenomenon continued into our species, but we need more information.

There is so much more to learn about particular behavioural instincts! We need to look at some species that will help us to understand the diversity of genetic transfer.

The European Cuckoo

3

A bird that baffles and entertains us is the European cuckoo. We ALL know that the cuckoo chooses a host bird's nest, lays an egg, and then disappears. *"Job done. End of all parental responsibilities for this year. Almost time to migrate."*

Furthermore, we know that after the egg hatches, the cuckoo chick, being much larger than other newly-hatched occupants, pushes them out of the nest, either to have all the space for itself or to ensure it receives all the food gathered by the host parents.

If a woman in a maternity hospital deliberately set out to achieve the same goal and have another woman rear her child (killing the foster mother's children in the process), there would be all hell let loose. Psychiatrists would be examining her and her child for years, trying to explain it. But we are all told the nice little story about the cuckoo when we are young, and it is all explained by the "i" word.

It is definitely against the maternal instinct, isn't it? All mothers are supposed to love their young, or at least care for them. Animals inherit a strong parental instinct or else how could the species survive?

So, why not the cuckoo? I mean, this sort of thing shouldn't happen. After all, it doesn't with humans.

Or does it? Cynics amongst you might point out that royalty and the aristocracy accepted the cuckoo syndrome as standard procedure centuries ago and have had their children raised by wet nurses, nannies, and boarding schools for centuries. Now other rich and not so rich people have jumped on the bandwagon and are doing the same thing. When you add on the use of surrogate mothers, I began to wonder who is copying whom?

I am tempted to explain the cuckoo theory in humans further, but let's get back to the bird.

Do we learn anything from studying the cuckoo and why it behaves as it does? I think it teaches us several interesting facts about "instinct."

Ignoring the trend

The natural inclination of birds is to find a mate, build a nest, lay eggs, hatch them, and work hard to rear the young until they are old enough to fend for themselves. Many species fight like tigers to defend their eggs and their young. (Wait until you walk near a plover's nest!) Charles Darwin claimed this was Nature's way of ensuring the survival of the species.

So, what happened to the European cuckoo? Its parental devotion is zero. It wants nothing to do with the constricting burdens of building nests, hatching, and rearing its progeny. Presumably it only lays eggs because it feels the biological need to mate, which results in an egg, which it has to get rid of in some poor, unsuspecting bird's nest because it can't (won't) (does not know how to) build a nest of its own and won't undertake the hassle of motherhood.

Besides being different and having its little story told to

children, the European cuckoo tells us a great deal about genetic inheritance and the power of instinct. It tells us that instinct can include passing on knowledge of **not doing** what others normally do:

- no inclination or inherited skills to construct a nest
- unwillingness to hatch eggs and nurture their young
- passing on the "instinct" in its young to push out the host bird's young, so that it can occupy the whole nest and receive all the food and attention of its 'foster parents.'

All of this begs the question, "*Why are they so different?*" Were they always like this? If so, it does not exactly follow the avian style of motherhood. So, in a major way, it bucks the trend for Darwin's theory that "effective maternal instincts ensure the survival of a species."

The ability to change an "instinct"

Did they *learn* to behave the way they do? The answer to this is important because, if they developed this behaviour over a period of time, it indicates that instincts in a species can *develop* or *change*, reinforcing the view that instincts are more flexible than some might imagine.

Although we *think* we all know how cuckoos behave, in fact only about 40 percent of the cuckoo family are *brood parasites* (lay eggs in a foster bird's nest). The majority of cuckoos world-wide build nests, lay eggs in them, and rear their young. The *European* cuckoo is the exception.

The North American variety is mainly "normal," but even so, quite a number of them are choosing to lay eggs in host birds' nests and then leave them. It is almost as if the *parental instinct* in this species has never been as strong as in other birds and, over time, there has been a leaning towards palming the job off to someone else. Why would this species act in this way?

The likely reason is that cuckoos have always been pretty poor at building nests. Compared to other species, their nests are generally rather primitive (some twigs on a branch, but no concave shape to retain eggs) and, as a species, cuckoos are rather haphazard as to where they build their nests: near the ground, high up a tree, or somewhere in the middle—certainly not highly functional nests like most species with specific nesting habits. So, it is possible that because they are not as successful as other birds, or more importantly, their inherited nest-building skills did not ensure maximum survival of eggs and young, the cuckoo (as a species) has evolved with a predisposition to not being "effective parents." and the European cuckoo has moved away from original parental behaviour for the species to become a brood parasite, thus ensuring the survival of the species in Europe. Over countless generations, this behaviour became *natural* (instinctive) for the European cuckoo.

Darwin was right after all. Successful animals are those that find *effective ways* to ensure that future generations survive.

The North American cuckoo is moving gradually into the parasitic phase already attained by its European cousin. It may take many thousands of years before cuckoos worldwide complete this transition. Nevertheless, it is an interesting example of how a species can **learn** to develop an instinct that, in turn, provides evidence against the "unthinking" theory.

A natural disinclination to be maternally efficient seemingly led the species to devise other means of disposing of the eggs. I will resist the temptation to add that they did it "to ensure the survival of their species" because we **all** "know" that birds are not capable of taking such a momentous leap forward in thought processes. But you have to admit, cuckoos must be much more intelligent than we might think. Their less-than-effective maternal instinct should have led to extinction. Instead, by means of lateral thinking, they produced an effective solution for the species.

The cuckoo's non-maternal behaviour also invites us to ask another relevant question.

Is the Maternal *Instinct* in animals really an "instinct"?

It is not just the cuckoo that can lack maternal feelings. Other birds reveal they have no interest in hatching and raising their young. Ducks frequently lay their eggs in another's nest. Why should this behaviour be so common? It would suggest that allocating time, energy, and devotion to rearing one's offspring is more a personal than instinctive act; that it is a *natural* activity for some animals whereas for others it is an unwanted and unnatural personal commitment that is to be avoided.

Other observers would claim that the laying of the eggs triggers the need to hatch them, and the arrival of the offspring arouses the desire to nurture them. They consider this a good example of conditioned (instinctive) behaviour.

Observation of animals, wild and domesticated, reveals that some females prove to be naturally excellent mothers, while many others will range from poor to bad.

The European cuckoo also demonstrates that an instinct not strongly implanted in a species (in this case nest building) could eventually lead to other so-called "instinctive behaviour" changes. That cuckoos found another solution to their difficulties in effectively producing the next generation is an impressive achievement in the animal kingdom. It also suggests they may be more intelligent and capable of more original thought than we might suspect.

"To ensure the survival of the species." How many times have we heard that comment! Strange how one minute the scientists

are describing *"unthinking, instinctive behaviour"* and then move straight into explaining how animals understand the requirements of the species and *take steps to ensure its survival*. I wish they would make up their minds!

Even humans don't consider *"survival of the species"* to be a prime reason for having children! The closest we get to it is, *"wanting to be needed"* (females) or *"leave something of myself here when I'm gone"* (males).

I think the main reason ensuring the continued existence of any and all species is not survival, but **pleasure**. The mating process is a driving biological force because animals enjoy doing it. That future generations are the result of it has been fortuitous for us all. The success of a species really depends on effective rearing processes after mating. After all, there is nothing more potentially endearing than seeing a young member of a species. Unfortunately after that, it is all hard work.

Darwin believed environmental factors led to habits forming gradually over time and only when behaviour had evolved a successful pattern did it eventually warrant the description "instinctive." It is summed up in the process of "evolve and multiply, let the strongest survive and the weakest die."

Secondly, we know that many species contain members that do not act according to the standard "species *parental* instinct." Some abandon their eggs, some abandon their young, and some let others hatch and raise them. This indicates that the inherited parental memory (if it exists) varies in strength.

I am of two minds. We could describe it as *"maternal instinct."* On the other hand, the individual's attraction to and ability at motherhood varies so much that *"maternal inclination"* seems more appropriate.

The European cuckoo's **non-maternal** behaviour is definitely instinctive. What do you think?

An issue that interests me, but will never be explained, is whether the cuckoo ever *thinks* about its lack of parental involvement? If it can knowingly change or create an instinct, it has to be something special.

I like to imagine it observing other birds hectically building nests and snuggling over their eggs (in all weathers) and then frantically becoming exhausted feeding the gobbling brood. Does it ponder as to whether it should do the same? Does it feel different? I like to think of the female cuckoo being amused by all the busy birds about it:

"Just look at them. They're all at it . . . building nests, snuggling down on the eggs for weeks to hatch their broods. My! Wait until you see them rushing around feeding the juveniles. Magic! Should I be doing the same thing? Should I? Nah! I'll stick to the old ways and lay my egg in that nest and then go on my holidays."

My thanks to the cuckoo for being such a stimulating and rewarding bird.

We now move on to other species that are even more revealing about the scope of inherited instincts. Let us look at **social insects**.

Social Insects

Termites offer a fascinating example of the potential for instinct at work. They are social insects (like ants, wasps, and bees), living and working together in structured communities—not unlike our own. They have evolved over more than two hundred million years. They build nests or colonies, the queen lays eggs, and these are looked after "with great care."

The queen begins laying eggs that produce *infertile workers*. They undertake the building of the nest, while the queen continues producing at the rate of up to a thousand eggs a day. Eventually, the nest will contain millions.

When the nest is big enough to need defending, the queen lays eggs that produce *soldier* termites, better equipped physically to undertake a defensive role.

When she deems the time and conditions to be appropriate, she will lay eggs to produce winged *fertile* males and females who will eventually leave the nest and endeavour to start their own colonies. A queen can live up to twenty years.

Nests can become huge (up to thirty feet tall) and contain millions of termites carrying out the functions needed to service this enormous community: builders and maintenance termites, nursery attendants, food gatherers, gardeners (producing a unique fungus as food) and, of course, the soldiers. The nest temperature is controlled at exactly 77°F (25°C) throughout the numerous passages and chambers. They live and work together for the good of the community. And all of this is achieved in darkness, as worker termites are mainly blind.

I resist the temptation to gush on about them. However, the functioning of the termite community is a joy to behold, and I would recommend anyone to buy a book or look on the Internet for more information on them or any other species of social insects. They can teach us a thing or two about serving our fellow citizens in a structured, harmonious and social society.

Do social insects teach us anything new about genetic inheritance?

I read one "expert's" comment that termites behave purely on instinct in their dark world as *they bump into each other until they reach a place where they end up doing something useful.* (That was the gist of it.) My reaction when I read his opinions was that I wished he had done exactly that himself!

Can you imagine a city of millions of blind people wandering about bumping into each other "looking" for something useful to do?

A termite colony is a social community that can run *smoothly and efficiently* for a period of up to twenty years (i.e., until the queen dies). Can you imagine the administrative direction and control a city of that number would require?

Our problem as human beings is that we tend we look **down** at an insignificant insect, when really we should be looking **up** at its level of achievement.

Constant maintenance of a thirty-foot structure with a myriad of passages and a network of essential activities requires more than "bumbling into each other." I would claim these insects could teach us a great deal about organisational skills. Others would dismiss it all as being instinctive, robotic behaviour that teaches us nothing. Let us examine this so-called "robotic" behaviour.

I have mentioned the great variety of work required in a termite colony. Such efficiency and dedication raises several important questions in my mind about genetic inheritance.

In a human situation, we would describe such behaviour as being loyal, dedicated, responsible, and selfless. Achieving harmony and efficiency of this standard would indicate a structured control system including awareness of requirement, allocation of resources, and discipline. It is difficult to think of insects in these terms, yet their performance warrants it. I could accept that their dedication to the cause could be instinctive. They are born with the desire to serve their community. But their success depends on multi-tasking. Are termites born with the ability to perform *all* those tasks on an *as required* basis, or are they born only with specific skills?

This is not a trivial or unimportant question if it helps us to understand a little more about genetic inheritance.

It could be that they are only able to complete specific tasks, like the soldier termites physically equipped to act as defenders, or the winged fertile termites equipped to fly off and hopefully form other communities.

On the other hand, it could be that the workers are born able to perform all community tasks. One might compare this with the Monarch butterfly inheriting knowledge of the whole migration, yet it would complete only about one fifth of the journey itself.

The queen is able to produce infertile workers or protectors at will. She can produce winged fertile termites when the conditions are right. She also produces fertile termites who function within the colony, and who would be capable of taking over as queen if she died. In fact, she is capable of producing the type and number of termites needed, on an "as and when required basis" to ensure that all aspects of the colony continue to function efficiently.

Would it not make sense, amongst the wingless fertile progeny, to produce a group of organisational leaders for the benefit of the smooth running of the nest? After all, loyalty and dedication will not maintain a community on their own. Twenty million occupants demand discipline, organisation, and leadership.

Perhaps the most intriguing question about the community must be the management of it. Social insects could not survive and prosper for millions of years by engaging in "random activities." That would be a chaotic and anarchic process. The termite colony is, most probably, a highly functional organism that contains more mysteries than we will ever know.

For those who would claim this is impossible, I would ask them for their scientific proof that it is impossible.

No doubt such views will be mocked. We do not wish to consider the possibility that inferior species, and certainly not ants and termites, possess better social skills than we have. We cannot conceive it—or, more than likely, we can't **prove** it, *ergo* we claim it does not exist.

Humans are happy to live in a world that believes they are the first to be so intelligent, the first to have such character and personality, the first to possess strong humanitarian feelings, the first to have developed effective communication and organisational skills, and so on.

It is as if, when Ape Man became Human, a metamorphosis took place producing so many *human* qualities in this wonderful, new species, none of which had ever existed before.

We even reinforce our superiority by referring to them as *human* qualities.

Admittedly, *Homo sapiens* are superior by virtue of brain capacity. But why not consider giving species who have survived for hundreds of millions of years the credit for possessing qualities of their own, which may or may not be all that distant from the ones we boast about?

This reluctance to credit insects with intelligence or organisational skills is comparable to a fifteen hundred-foot giant gazing down on two hundred thousand Chinese workers building a dam with their bare hands during Chairman Mao's rule and expressing amazement that so many little creatures running all over the place, bumping into each other, could manage to build a dam without any evidence of a plan or coordination.

I repeat a sentence given earlier that random activity on the part of individuals does not achieve anything significant. Give a hundred squaddies (soldiers) a spade each and tell them to build a structure (without direction or a plan) and you will end up with a hundred squaddies standing in a field holding spades!

Why do so many "scientists" object to any "humanising" of certain sections of the animal kingdom? Such human descriptions as loving and loyal, hardworking, devoted, and intelligent can be applied to dogs and horses. Why should attributing such qualities be ridiculous for the lower orders of the kingdom?

Perhaps it is because we can see the proof of its existence in dogs and horses. It just happens to be less discernible and verifiable in insects. We never hesitate to describe some humans as *behaving like animals*. It is time we accepted that *animals behave more like humans*.

Why am I going on about these qualities in termites, ants, and other social insects? Because I admire their work ethic, their loyalty to the community, the intelligence they display in such abundance, and their sacrifice for the good of their communities. Humans should watch and learn.

Furthermore, they did not acquire such commendable personal qualities from advanced training opportunities within the community after birth. **They were born with them.**

The species implants recognisable qualities at birth and personal traits that contribute significantly to the efficient running and survival of their colony.

Now we are reaching a point where we are able to summarise what has long been dismissively called *instinct*, as a many-faceted genetic *inheritance* that, amongst other things, encompasses:

- physical skills (building webs and nests, etc.)
- transfer of other knowledge (e.g., migration skills)
- passing on knowledge of something that has not been personally experienced (e.g., *Monarch* butterflies born with complete knowledge of a five-month migration when each generation will only live through four weeks of that journey)
- behaviour patterns that contradict that of other avian species (European cuckoo)
- instinctive abilities in species may vary in effectiveness (e.g., a duck abandoning its eggs in another's nest)
- inheriting personal qualities, such as *character* and *temperament* (e.g., in dogs/horses) with a predisposition to be loving or fierce, intelligent and loyal
- compulsive behaviour (e.g., salmon breeding behaviour)
- inheriting organisational skills capable of administering millions of individuals in a multi-task situation.

The list goes on. No one denies this impressive range of abilities exists in the animal kingdom. They are either genetically transmitted or learned after birth (which would have to involve "learning and teaching processes" and all that implies). If it did involve teaching and learning, that would be even more mind-boggling. How would the scientific world explain that?

To my mind, the behaviour of social insects allows us to contemplate animal behaviour akin to desirable human behaviour, and it seems likely that such traits are inherited.

Social insects remind us that there are species whose existence would call for direction and control, and a more sophisticated level of communication skills. They are an example of members of the animal kingdom acting in, and serving the needs of, large social communities. They work for and with other members of their community. They create and maintain complex structures that serve and protect their communities for many years. If they do not convince you that they inherit numerous social skills, they should at least make you wonder how on earth they manage to achieve what they do.

They focus our attention as to the requirements of a structured community of millions of members. We either subscribe to the view that "termites bump into each other in the dark, randomly allocating themselves a daily task" or, while accepting we have no scientific proof, deduce, and conclude that termites, ants, and bees are, not only worthy of being called social insects, but they deserve to be recognised as being highly organised insects that exist harmoniously with each other, with all that entails.

After all, it is we humans who describe them as **social** insects.

Communication in the Animal Kingdom

The structured communities of the termite and other social species highlight the probable need and existence of another significant ability in the animal kingdom—*communication skills*.

Until recent decades, the scientific community has not paid much attention to studying animal skills and behaviour. They have also dismissed the possibility of them having any advanced communication skills.

Oh, they condescendingly accepted that certain animals make basic sounds to warn of danger, to attract mates, to intimidate competitors, etc., but efficient communication was not on the agenda. Perhaps they were confused between the terms *language* skills and *communication* skills.

Humans have many forms of communication, only one of which is the spoken language. We have the vocal chords and the brainpower to create a complicated, detailed language system.

Because other species do not to have this combination, it has been concluded that they can only communicate at the most basic of levels, and certainly nothing like "sentences," coherent ideas, or "speech." Furthermore, as it was assumed that, as much of their activity is instinctive, there would be no need for more sophisticated methods of communication.

One example of this is the *scientific* explanation of the bee's *bum waggling* language. We have all heard of that. My reaction to the theory that the bee returns to the hive and waggles its backside energetically to reveal all the details of a new source of nectar (direction, distance, and quantity) was that it reminded me of *Pavlov's* experiment with dogs. Pavlov encouraged acceptance of the concept of conditioned behaviour in animals, and the bee bum waggle theory encapsulated the view of primitive animals having primitive communication techniques.

I think it is fair to add that not a great deal of serious scientific research has been undertaken on this subject.

The animal kingdom has proved itself capable of satisfying its needs. Humans have the gift of eyesight that serves us well in our daily lives. If we lose that sight, we are able to compensate to some extent by considerably improving other senses such as touch, smell, or hearing. We improve our senses to make our lives better.

There is plenty of evidence to suggest that other species develop essential personal abilities to a high level to assist them in their task of surviving. Hawks that search for small prey on the ground while flying high have developed eyesight far better than ours to make that possible. And species that hunt at night have developed more effective night vision.

A principal need of a herd of grazing animals is access to grassland. We might feel justified in thinking that, with their restricted range of activity, whatever communication skills they possess would be limited.

But dare we be so arrogant as to claim that millions of multitasking termites thriving in single communities over a period of two hundred million years were not capable during that time of developing their one major requirement—an effective communication and control system? Developing and maintaining a major enterprise consisting of millions of individuals with a range of skills and activities cannot survive if it functions as a random venture. Whether in human or insect situations, it would demand planning, direction, control, and expertise.

Don't dwell on the fact that we are talking about termites. Concentrate on what is being achieved and what is required to achieve it.

It may be difficult to prove they have achieved a high level of communication skills, but let not lack of scientific proof prevent us from using logic and objective commonsense. To deny its existence is like claiming that snakes and fish could not move efficiently because they have no legs, and then only acknowledging they could when it was seen how those species had compensated.

Consider by which process the termite queen **knows** that more workers or soldiers are required, or the seasonal changes that signal the time for producing winged termites. Is a queen all-seeing and all-knowing in her location deep within the nest or is it not unreasonable to conjecture that she is constantly informed or advised of the population needs of the colony.

I am interested in this communication conundrum because, once again, it raises the question, *"If they do have communication skills, do they **learn** them or are they **born with** them?"* I ask myself this question on so many aspects of animal behaviour because either answer is amazing.

If they are born with the skills, it is another demonstration of the scope of genetic inheritance. If they learn them, then that involves a teaching process that, in turn, requires effective communication.

There is a difference between what we call *language* and the art of communicating. We imagine "language" to be words, sentences, and grammar, and we cannot imagine lower forms of life as being able or intelligent enough to have a "language" of their own. This is so patronising when one realises that, over the ages, different groups of *Homo sapiens,* large and small, around the world independently developed their own highly individualised spoken and written systems. We may not understand them, but we have to accept that they are effective in the correct environment.

Communication includes all forms of imparting information to others. Humans not possessing the ability to speak have survived and prospered.

Humans delight in teaching domestic animals to respond to words and sounds. Sheep dogs learn to respond to whistles and horses are taught to do dressage.

We will readily admit that whales and dolphins indulge in underwater communication, or that birds and animals have warning calls when danger is imminent. We can hear those. Besides, we are told they are only "primitive" signals.

The newly born deer remains hidden in the grass when danger lurks and remains still even when its mother draws off the predator. That is brilliant. Was it born with that defensive instinct or did its mother teach it to it?

Observing packs of hunting animals, such as lions, wild dogs, and wolves demonstrates hierarchy and effective communication. We even use the term *pecking order* to indicate one's position in a group. Study any group of birds and we will soon become aware of which are the dominant ones.

When countless millions of red killer ants go on the move in the jungle, is a decision made and communicated to the millions of ants? It would seem so. Otherwise, each one would have to decide to "go walkies" at the same time.

I return to the question as to what are the main criteria for believing that communication skills at all levels of the animal kingdom are far greater than we give them credit for:

(1) It does not seem possible that species that have survived intact for so long in controlled and structured societies do not have means of communication that are highly effective for them.

(2) Creatures on land, sea, and air have the intelligence to learn new skills from humans. Surely over millions of years that same intelligence has enabled them to evolve their own effective forms of communication with each other. Do we honestly believe that we are the only species on earth with effective means of communication?

As intelligent people, let us concede that there must be some degree of effective communication in the insect world, and the animal world generally, even if they are far removed from our own. We need to study the animal kingdom far more seriously to understand the scope of their magical skills, if only to see what indicators are there for understanding human behaviour.

We have all watched a line of ants scurrying along the ground to and from a food source. They occasionally stop and seem to communicate to ants going the other way, as if they were giving a greeting. Why would they do that? If they are following a scented trail, they can't be asking the way or enquiring whether there is any food left. It is not a major issue but, for me, it is interesting because it appears to be a form of *social communication*. It could be for two reasons.

– Perhaps ant A recognizes ant B and gives him a greeting.
– Perhaps ant C is a "friend" of ant D and has a few words.

Is that train of thought childish? If so, why do they stop? The interval of time may appear insignificant to us, but imagine how many heartbeats of time it takes for us to greet or converse with someone. An ant's "conversation" would take a fraction of that time.

Is it so difficult to accept that the "communication" skills of insects must be effective to sustain the multi-tasking essential to their communities? If they can inherit memories containing migratory knowledge, directional skills, homing skills, and other practical skills in their tiny brains, inheriting communication skills of the species should be a doddle!

Years ago, I was discussing the function of memory transfer with my son-in-law and he asked me how I visualised the brain's process for receiving and retaining information. The question caught me by surprise and made me realise I had never thought about it. I had just assumed, in my usual non-scientific style, that a memory bank was like some glorified mental tape recorder that stored memories that could be accessed when needed.

He then explained that the brain had billions of nerve ends (*neurons*) that were linked by trillions of *neural circuits* interacting with each other as they dealt with all mental processes. I tried to imagine that, but gave up, deciding just to accept it as the original microchip (and I don't know how that works, either).

It is not difficult to realise how complicated the mind and memory is, because it is capable of such wonderful achievements, as demonstrated by the smallest of instincts. If they have similar, but less advanced circuits, in their tiny brains, then perhaps that fact helps us to understand and accept the mysteries of genetic transfer.

Because insufficient time has been devoted to studying the range of abilities of other species in the animal kingdom, let us not jump to too many negative conclusions about them.

After all, most of them will still be here long after our species has disappeared.

Mysteries of Migration 6

Many animals make annual migrations seeking better food supplies and water, or avoiding difficult weather conditions. Perhaps they need to be in a place of plenty to produce and feed their offspring. Such migrations are built into their survival patterns and have become part of their behaviour.

We speak of the *mystery* elements of migration when we experience difficulty in understanding and explaining how little bird brains, fish brains, and other sub-human brains can perform such momentous deeds.

We try to explain how salmon and turtles travel thousands of miles to specific locations to breed. We can marvel how butterflies and birds migrate along lengthy fixed routes. It is easy to explain *why* they set out on these journeys. The mystery rests in the *how*.

Bird banding over the years has proved that many birds migrate back and forth to the same wintering spots each year. It is therefore tempting to believe that the older, experienced birds lead the way and teach younger birds the route. But in some species, adult birds do not migrate at the same time as the juveniles. I first came across this in Suffolk, England. A flock of birds gradually assembled on telephone wires ready to migrate. I commented that it was a bit soon for the young to be undertaking such a journey, and was told by a local that the young were not yet strong enough. They had to wait a while before they could undertake the trip. I wondered how they had the conviction to attempt the journey and the ability to complete it on their own.

Searching for an explanation, I came across theories about *"birds use the sun and stars to obtain compass directions, at the same time requiring a map of the night sky and an understanding of the pull of the earth's magnetic field. Because of the dangers of the journey, they also needed to take weather into account as well as utilising favourable winds."*

I expected it to be followed by, ***"Oh, and they need a navigator's licence, an Honours Degree in mathematics, geography, and climatology."***

Assessments of their migratory abilities seem to have changed from being robotic, unthinking animals to navigating geniuses.

If migrations of a large group of juveniles are blessed with the fanatical enthusiasm of a religious zealot, how daunting must be the migration of the young cuckoo. Nurtured by foster parents, and with no adult cuckoos to follow, it migrates alone to its ancestral wintering grounds in the tropics, before returning single-handedly to northern Europe to seek out a mate among its kind. That is really spooky. Think of all the *"gifts of inheritance"* required for it to complete those tasks unaided. The only conclusion must be they inherit the whole package: to kick other juveniles out of the foster bird's nest, the urge and knowledge for migration when the time is right, and knowing it has to lay its eggs in a "foster nest."

It is generally assumed that birds follow the same migratory journey each year and know that route. There may be more to it than that. Banded birds on migration from North America to South America have been blown off course and landed in the UK. Bird fanciers there have caught them and from their tags were able to write to the scientists in America telling them what had happened and the date they were released again. It has been known for a bird released in the UK to return to the States before that notification letter was delivered.

This anecdote tells us that the bird's knowledge could not have been limited to its normal migratory route. It also possessed the ability to return to its base from a different continent. Perhaps such homing skills are not limited to pigeons. My respect for the natural abilities of birds increases all the time.

The wonder of migration is not just how they do it. The wonder is that they *do* it. The magic is that whatever means they use to achieve their goals, they inherit it. Many call it instinct. I call it *gifts:* phenomenal powers handed down through evolution.

To me, the incredible magic surrounding bird or butterfly migrations is not *how* they achieve them, perhaps because I feel we may never know for sure. Perhaps the true message to us is that we have no idea of, and would never believe, the true magic of the animal kingdom.

Salmon travel enormous distances to reach the river in which they wish to spawn; turtles do the same to reach the same beach for laying their eggs; some species of frogs or crabs assemble in millions to mate and reproduce, as do jelly fish. They know when and where to go. I understand why they go (because they have the need to mate). This aspect of instinctive behaviour— and the knowledge involved to execute it—has never been adequately explained. Since it has taken millions of years of evolution to reach its current state of success, migratory behaviour is not going to be explained with a few human-based ideas. All we can do is sit back with a drink in our hands and watch in amazement as the television screen shows us how amazing they are.

I pity the dedicated ethologist (person studying the behaviour of animals) who endeavours to find explanations for some of the mysteries.

It all goes to prove that the minds of small creatures inherit so much that is inexplicable, and so much that would be unbelievable if we were not able to witness their mysterious achievements for ourselves. If we did not have visible proof, we would never believe the magical "myths" of the animal kingdom.

We ought to seriously ponder such matters when we come to consider the potential mysteries that might or must be contained in the human brain.

Parental Responsibility in Animals

Thousands of species on land, in the sea, and the air have evolved individual approaches to successfully bringing forth the next generation. That they continue to exist is proof that their methods work.

Frogs, turtles, and salmon are a few examples of species leaving their young to survive on their own. Because I am still seeking more information about instinct, I am interested mainly in the capability of animals that nurture their young.

We are all aware of the birth processes of domesticated animals and wild animals. Their stages of mating, conception, birth, and nurturing are ones we recognise and accept.

It all seems kind of normal and straightforward, despite the possibility of difficulties. One could almost conclude that the whole process from mating onwards is biologically natural. Yet we regularly hear talk of *instinctive behaviour* regarding parenthood. Certain aspects of parenting can include behaviour that appears to be instinctive, but is the individual animal's dedication to parenting closer to being a natural response to caring for one's young? Did this behaviour have to develop as an instinct or was its strong presence in the species a major factor in the process of surviving?

One can be confident that specific behaviour is inherited. What of the nurturing part? Is feeding a hungry brood instinctive or just a biological response to hungry mouths?

Is defending your young against potential attackers and placing yourself in danger to protect them instinctive or natural?

Such questions are important whether the answers are *natural* or *instinctive*, because it reveals a little more as to what can be passed on to the next generation.

If the answer is **instinctive,** then we know that such personal qualities as concern for the young and lack of concern for oneself when faced with danger can be inherited.

This explains how even animals that fear the lion will try to defend their young against them.

If such behaviour were deemed **natural,** then it would not be present in all members of the species. Presumably, some in the species would immediately abandon their young to their fate, while others may want to defend the young, but back down out of fear.

Either way, it does highlight the presence of a strong desire to raise and protect.

It reminds me of a salmon's instinctive mental need to get to the proper place for laying its eggs. It raises the image of a soldier desperately crossing a huge desert to pass on vital military intelligence. We would describe such an achievement as dedicated and heroic.

I am tempted to use such descriptive words as devotion and determination to describe such parental dedication. You may dismiss it all as purely "instinctive" behaviour with nothing to do with devotion or dedication, but would you also describe a woman risking life and limb to save her children from a burning house as being purely instinctive with no emotional input?

There is another side to parenting that is also self-evident. We know that species generally renowned for caring after their young also contain poor mothers, reluctant mothers, neglectful mothers, and bad mothers. Those of us who have kept pets are likely to have observed these differing levels of parenting.

After the young have been delivered, the mother takes control of events. In an ideal situation, she would possess all the right attitudes for the care of her young. As this part of parenting is far more personal, the standards of behaviour are likely to be more flexible in performance.

Does that prove that this part of parenting is not inherited, but is down to the personal attitudes and abilities of the individual animal? Even if that were so, the animal would have been *born with* its attitudes and abilities to parenting, whether they were excellent, mediocre, poor, or non-existent?

Inexperience can play its part in poor mothering to begin with, but abandoning the young is not uncommon in the wild. Presumably the mother is not lazy, and does not *choose* to be a less than perfect mother. One can only surmise that she possesses neither the desire nor the ability to nurture.

It also proves how clever the European cuckoo was. It came up with a solution for the effective production of the next generation in spite of lacking the necessary skills for mother-hood. One thing we can say is that its **lack of** avian maternal feelings is instinctive because it is common to the whole species.

Just as there can be lack of maternal instinct, so there can be an abundance of it—so much so that adults of one species will adopt the young of another.

We have heard of cats feeding puppies, and dogs feeding piglets. Perhaps this was due to the mother having excess milk. But when a lioness nurtures and protects an abandoned young deer, then maternal instinct has moved to a different plain, showing the potential strength of maternalism in animals. Such a lioness must have been a loner (because no male lion would be daft enough to allow such behaviour). Had she been forced to leave the pride because she was infertile? She must have had a heart full of caring.

For me, one of the most heart-warming aspects of parenting in the wild is that, no matter how good, bad, or indifferent they are as a parent, they are not judged by others. There's no need for guilt or feelings of inadequacy. We could learn from that.

The Importance of Lineage 8

Inherited knowledge and its resulting behaviour have long played a major role in the survival of a species. They have been the dominant factors determining whether a species had a future.

But all members of a species are not cloned robots. In the wild, they look alike, and seemingly behave and survive together, but they are also individuals with their individual character, temperament, and "personality" (or should that be *animality*?).

I do not make that statement based on personal experience in jungles and plains with wild animals, but one does not have to be a genius to know that, in the same species, some will be strong-willed and leaders, while others are happy to follow, and some will be fierce, while others are gentle, etc. It is significant that character and temperament are mental, not physical, traits.

We will accept that their collective appearance and instincts are specifically associated with their species. Just as interesting and informative is whether their personal lineage within that species also makes a significant contribution to other personal *"qualities"* which do not qualify as "instincts." (I have previously stated that, whereas all instincts are genetically inherited, all that is genetically inherited need not be classed as instinct.)

This is important because, if such personal qualities in animals as character and temperament, determination and leadership, and being caring and maternalistic can be determined at birth, it further demonstrates the influence of lineage in genetic inheritance.

We would be moving away from perceiving genetic inheritance as only a provider of physical characteristics and *"instinctive behaviour."* Genetic inheritance would not then be considered merely as a "**survival tool that ensured the continuation of the species.**" It would also be considered as a natural, evolutionary consequence of conception and birth. It would mean that an animal could pass on personal qualities that belonged to itself, even its parents, or others in its line. Such a concept needs to be examined more closely.

Are genetic inheritance and lineage a combination?

Wherever there are wild animals in large numbers, they consist of leaders and followers. There can also be a clear pecking order accepted by all.

Is it purely a matter of the strongest being the leader, and the followers are weaker, or does a leader need a lineage that endows it with strength, willpower, and presence?

It may be easier if we look at domesticated animals. A litter of pups growing up will contain boisterous and timid ones, as well as active and lazy ones. They have all been there together, yet they demonstrate a range of "character" between them.

Breeders certainly believe that lineage matters. They maintain meticulous records of an animal's ancestry to be referred to when selecting the mates of their prize animals.

Owners believe it, too, because they pay large sums of money to buy quality pedigree animals. And they are not paying purely for perfect appearance of the breed. Intelligence is just as important in certain breeds. Pedigree dogs are carefully paired to produce a litter with the desired physical and mental qualities.

The benefit of lineage awareness is that the breeder has much greater confidence that the pairing of selected animals will produce the desired qualities in the progeny.

The same applies to racehorses. Fortunes are paid to have good mares mated with proven champions, even though there is no guarantee that the outcome will be a future champion! As in all things involving genetic transfer, there is no certainty that all the desired attributes will be passed on, but quality mated with quality increases the odds of success. Many racehorses have appearance and speed, but only champions have that special mental stamina to beat everyone.

Royalty and the aristocracy have long adhered to the concept of lineage. *"Breeding will always come to the fore."* Unfortunately, this belief is somewhat misplaced because the one essential lineage ingredient for effective breeding is personal performance, not position in society. Knowing how to behave before one's peers is an acquired skill, not an innate personal quality.

If one were to buy a cocker spaniel as a pet, it would be in the knowledge that it would be a friendly, loving, greedy little thing, and a new member of the household.

Certain breeds have been created as fighting animals. They will act as family pets if treated properly, or become vicious animals if the owner encourages it. Many people are extremely wary of such dogs because, even though they may have been brought up as a pet, their innate, vicious capability can appear with disastrous results. Many such examples have been documented.

When I was young, my family dog was a Kerry Blue terrier that would go berserk, rushing forward with head to the ground snarling when anyone (non-family) approached the house via the side gate. Bin men and coal men would tip toe up to the front door and ring the doorbell to check on the whereabouts of the dog before daring to open the back gate.

One day a policeman arrived at the house with a serious complaint by a passerby that our dog had viciously attacked him in the street. Fortunately, when the policeman rang the bell, the dog was inside the house, where he was always like a pussycat. The policeman stroked and patted his head, and the dog accepted it all with a wagging tail (because my mother was standing there).

"*Well,*" said the policeman. "*If he did bite him, he must have been provoked.*" And off he went.

It also demonstrates how an animal can behave completely differently when in or out of its comfort zone.

We talk of qualities of character and temperament being bred into animals. Where does that leave **personality?** Can that also be transferred?

Personality is the projected image of the individual as perceived by others. It cannot exist on its own. Character and temperament are the foundations, but personality is how the animal presents these attributes.

For those who laugh at such an idea, there are many animal owners who will swear their pets do have personalities.

I agree it may be difficult to imagine buffaloes or ants having "personalities." The word *person* implies *human*. How can that apply to animals?

One definition of personality is *"the sum total of all the behavioural and mental characteristics by means of which an individual is recognised as being unique."* I chose this one because it could range from an animal devoid of memorable qualities to one that is charismatic.

Personality is the window to their character and temperament. Millions of animal owners will testify to the fact that their pets have so-called "human" qualities of love and devotion, of character and personality, and of sensitivity and awareness. They justifiably become members of the family and when they die, the loss can be felt as greatly as the loss of a friend or family member.

Once again, I may be accused of "humanising" animals. It is not my intention. It is just that I believe that living things are not robots. They must make individual contributions to their environment. Because we cannot verify such ideas does not make them unrealistic or unreasonable.

Furthermore, if these "human" qualities are present, then much of what they are must be due to inheritance and lineage. Otherwise, we enter the realm of assessing how and when the character differences between individual animals develop. Environment may influence them, but they are there long before external influences get to work on them.

Inability to provide scientific proof of this fact does not deter me. If I were an ant looking up at the *massive* human giants above me, I would want to be the ant philosopher who claimed, **"I am, therefore I think"** Of course, such an ant statement would be wasted on humans!

I don't know whether I am asking too much when I ask you to accept my idea that individual members of the so-called *lower* species have some form of individual character and personality. I keep mentioning it because I find it hard to accept that humans "invented" the ability to love and care for others; that Man created the personality factor; and that it was people who discovered qualities like loyalty and dedication.

How strange it is that all good qualities in us are deemed to be *human qualities*, yet bad qualities like brutality and killing are classed as *behaving like an animal*.

My final thoughts on the question of lineage move from pedigree animals to so-called *rainbow* variety, the result of random mating between breeds. Such mongrels possess most, if not more, of the qualities of the pedigree ones. Their unmonitored lineage creates them with great character and temperament, skills and personality, and love and devotion, all engineered by Nature and not humans. What is more, such animals cost much less. Pedigree may influence appearance, but it is lineage that will provide important qualities. **Where would we be without that basic truth?**

Choosing Mates

Evolution cannot be said to lack a sense of humour. It would have been so easy for different genders to come together, mate, and leave Nature to do the rest. Instead, it introduced choice and considerable variety into the selection process.

Methods of selecting mates vary greatly from species to species. Somebody explained this as being necessary to enable a female to "recognise" a male of its own species. This implies that a female cannot recognise a male without some courtship ritual. I find that rather odd, particularly as the males tend to be more colourful and noticeable.

There is the believable theory that females in the species were dominant in defining mating rituals when selection was required. Whatever stimulated them in the selection process became the preferred mating ritual for that species.

We can ignore the rather mundane process of numerous males and females coming together at the same time with an apparent random engaging in mating, and examine a few different mate selection rituals in the animal world.

Do they choose a mate to ensure the future of the species?

As so much animal behaviour is attributed to the instincts of the species, *scientists* advise us that reasons for animals engaging in mate selection include guaranteeing the best possible offspring. This may be true to a certain extent, but it could include wanting progeny who will possess the same qualities that first attracted the female to the male.

This viewpoint appears to raise the biological awareness of animals above that of human beings. I must confess that the future of *Homo sapiens* was not top of my list on my honeymoon, and there was a time in our past when humans did not know that mating produced the next generation.

Animals have biological needs that have to be satisfied. When mating ensues, the consequences are offspring, which eventually become adults, and if the process is then repeated successfully, **that** is the future of a species. It revolves around sex.

When a new male lion takes over a pride, it will kill all young, nursing cubs. He does this, not because he wants future offspring *to be of his seed*, but because he wants to mate with the lionesses as soon as possible. He is aware that when the cubs are dead, the lionesses will quickly come into season again and he will be able to mate with them.

The females of a species play a predominant part in the selection of mates. Selection rituals are many and varied.

The Protector

In species where the males build up a harem of females, it is natural that the strongest males have the largest harems. We are told the females "are happy with this system because it ensures that good genes will be passed on to their young and ensure the strength and future of their line." I am not convinced by this human argument. I'll tell you why.

It is advocating that animals like deer and sea lions think about such subjects as the gene pool and the species. I am more inclined to believe that the females think less about the species and more of appreciating what a big, strong boy she is mating with and, even more likely, how she is attracted by the fact he will be capable of *protecting* her and her kin from predators and unwanted suitors. This is the *"He will look after and protect me"* syndrome.

Take animals with magnificent displays of antlers. If the males are impressed by them, the females will certainly be— definitely a case of *"the bigger the better."* Never fails.

The Home Provider

Then there is the *"Will he provide me with a good home?"* type, as with the weaver bird. The male constructs a hanging nest to attract a female. Building one of these is a work of art in itself. The nest requires a strong tie to the branch and may include several entrances to confuse potential predators. When completed, a female is invited to inspect it. She will test it thoroughly and, if she is not convinced it is secure enough to hold her and her offspring, she will leave to inspect another male's offering. And remember, the unsuccessful male cannot go to evening classes to learn how to make a better one!

The Pretty Boy

Then we have peacocks and other exotic tropical birds. You've seen them on TV prancing about in front of the females. Some of their antics are incredible as they lower their heads, preen themselves and ruffle their feathers to impress the onlooker. I always imagine the female giving them marks out of ten for poise, style, originality, effort, and entertainment . . .

and then making up her mind. There doesn't appear to be any "Will he protect me or provide me with a good home" approach with these species. It seems to be a lot of *pretty boy* routine. Well, some are bound to go for that, aren't they? Yes, but will it last?

The Artist

I am impressed by the male *bower* bird artistically placing objects of different shapes, colours, and textures around the entrance to his nest site. This is inventive. *"Look how original I am and keen to satisfy your needs"* is the theme. Bower birds clear the area they are preparing for display. Items on display can include fruit, feathers, shells, bleached bones, coloured stones, etc.

It is fascinating how the females of this species came to encourage such behaviour. It certainly beats bringing a dozen roses.

The Provider

Some species consist of male birds sticking to basics and bringing food to the female to show how he will provide for her and her brood. I suppose we could classify this as the *"Let me take you out to dinner"* approach.

The Serenader

Then there are birds that attract mates by singing away and even mimicking sounds and calls of other birds. Their courtship involves the male going through his repertoire of bird calls and other sounds to impress the lady. (This must be the musical version of the exotic feather display) . . . the *"blind them with science"* routine.

The "Rest of my Life" Approach

I suppose the swans offer us the *"I have fallen in love and want to be with you for the rest of my life"* routine. They are wonderful examples of long-term partnerships. Sadly, even amongst swans, a small percentage of pairs split up. Just proves that no species is perfect in marital terms.

The Independent One

Let us not forget those independent, self-reliant female birds that make their own nests, find their own food, hatch the eggs, and nurture their broods. They only need the males to satisfy one essential requirement and they will attract a number of mates to ensure it is met. Their main mating requirement is that the bird is male. Good for you, girl!

I am sure the list could go on and on, but I have given enough to demonstrate that the animal kingdom has evolved with many and varied mate selection procedures. The drab female (for camouflage while nesting) frequently does the choosing. She does not have to put make up on and wear her best dress. As in all species, the males are driven by something other than appearances, and they are desperate to get it. All they expect from the female is an indication of approval. Nature is truly a wonderland.

Why so many mating rituals?

Is it really necessary to have so many courting rituals in the animal kingdom? One would have thought that the sex drive would have been sufficient to encourage males and females of a species to meet and mate without all the rigmarole of courting. Male meets available female when she is ready to mate, gives her the nod, and the rest is history. Survival of the species, too!

I find it reassuring that rituals can be based on logic, common sense, practicality, sensitivity, or just plain lust. They also reveal the independent pathways of each species.

As all these successful species independently adopted such a variety of mate selection processes, it makes one wonder which of these mate selection processes could have been passed on in the evolutionary development of later species.

Sexuality in the Animal Kingdom

It is easy to assume that sexuality in the animal kingdom would be straightforward—"*All males and females mate with the intention of producing the next generation and ensuring the survival of the species.*" Evolution has dictated how they go about it, and television companies produce wonderful nature programmes for our enlightenment about animal behaviour, including birth, mating, and death.

I cannot honestly recall hearing a Nature TV commentator comment that animal sexuality is extremely varied or that they engage in it primarily because they *enjoy* it. Time and again there was mention of *survival* and *the species*.

How come the animal kingdom is supposed to have known about it for millions of years? I'll give them credit for many abilities but, knowledge of the reproductive process? It was not too far back in our history that even humans did not connect copulation with population.

Would you be shocked to learn that homosexual and bisexual behaviour is rampant in the animal kingdom? Research has found they exist in over fifteen hundred species tested so far. The conclusion was that this must be the case in most species.

How can one explain such a phenomenon in Nature? What

could be the point of it? It only results in a waste of potential providers of future generations.

If sexual activity exists to ensure the continuity of life, what factors lead to such diverse sexual inclinations in animals?

"Sex for survival of the species?"

Such a statement is ridiculous, if only because it endows all animals with wisdom they do not possess.

Sex is for pleasure because Nature evolved on the basis that an act of giving pleasure was the best way of ensuring that it took place—as often as possible. Those species that successfully engaged in sex, and developed efficient methods of producing the next generation, were the species that survived.

Why are there so many sexual orientations?

Eyes are to see; legs are for walking; sexual organs are for procreation. One would think it illogical for evolution to have produced numerous sexual orientations when only one leads to procreation. Nevertheless, it is the situation that exists, and it occurs naturally.

It can't have anything to do with controlling the numbers of offspring produced because Nature employs other methods for that. Small mammals have large litters frequently because they are an important link in the food chain of predators, so a few need to survive to adulthood. Elephants, which live for decades, will only have one calf every few years. Animals even have the objectivity not to feed weak offspring when food is limited.

If they were not created for procreation, what was the purpose in them having a non-productive sexual orientation? It does not seem efficient, and Nature normally tries its best to be efficient. Well, there was never a purpose, just an outcome.

Might one form of sexual activity be more pleasurable than

another? My conclusion on this point, albeit offered without any scientific proof, is that, whichever way sexual activity is conducted, the participants must all enjoy considerable sexual gratification.

There has been no research, to my knowledge, proving that selection of sexuality in animals is by individual choice. Once again, that is unlikely because it would imply that, at sexual maturity, a particular animal considers its *options*.

Can anyone possibly imagine the farcical situation of an animal trying to determine which sexual inclination it should choose? *"Shall I opt for traditional mating with the opposite sex, with all that implies, or go for sexual gratification with members of my own gender? Possibly non-productive but, nevertheless, reports on it are promising. I just can't make up my mind, so I will have sex with both genders."*

Is sexuality inherited?

I have never heard human condemnation of diversity in animal sexuality. Perhaps the diversity of sexual behaviour in the animal kingdom is not widely known by the public or religious authorities. Or, if it is, they have dismissed it as an "animal thing" therefore not significant or worthy of comment.

When one becomes aware of the diversity of sexual inclinations amongst animals, it is normal to consider whether it is a **natural** phenomenon in Nature—a natural phenomenon in a natural earth that many claim was created by a higher power.

Having pontificated about it being *natural,* does that mean sexual orientation *is* instinctive in animals?

It has often been described as such, and because so much animal activity is considered to be instinctive, it could be accepted as a reasonable statement. *But is it?*

Courting behaviour can definitely be classed as instinctive because all males and females in the species behave in a similar manner when searching for and choosing mates.

If all members of a species were born with heterosexual tendencies, there would be more grounds for claiming it to be instinctive. A species *instinct* is passed on to all members, even though its impact on an individual is known to vary in some cases.

Could it be an instinct that is not always 100 percent perfect in transfer, resulting in the majority being heterosexual and the remainder possessing some other orientations?

If we keep following that train of thought, we will be clutching at straws. *"Sexual orientation cannot be instinctive behaviour when there is such diversity in a species."*

So, sexuality can be described as many things, but not instinctive.

So, what is it?

It is confusing when we say they are *born* with their sexuality, but it is not an instinct. Does that not conflict with what I wrote earlier that instinct means *"born with, inherited."*? Yes and no. One can be born with a hereditary disease, but we cannot call it an instinctive disease because all members of the species do not have it.

If it is natural in animals, but not instinctive, what is it? Some medical professionals believe sexuality is determined by a complicated mixture of physical and mental factors, which are not fully understood.

The facts are that a percentage of male animals display no desire or interest in the females of the species, and vice versa. Yet they still possess sexual urges that need to be met.

Basically, the be all and end all of sexual orientation is the gender to which one is attracted sexually.

If homosexuality and bisexuality are evident in animals, and there is irrefutable evidence that they are, then this principle of attraction must also apply throughout the animal kingdom.

What causes that *attraction*? Remember, this is different from choosing a mate. Personal attraction to a gender needs to be determined before any mating selection takes place.

Does that strike you as difficult to imagine? A sexually active, large, hairy bison looking at a sexually ready female bison in season and not being interested? But it happens.

Research has shown that one in six rams declines the chance to mate with sheep in mating sessions.

Sexual orientation cannot be a biologically-based decision because hormones and genitalia are the basis of the physical need for sex. They may influence *promiscuity*, but not gender attraction.

Many animals use secretions and scents to publicise that they are ready to mate, but again, this has nothing to do with sexual inclinations Medical, professional opinion definitely includes *mental* influence in sexual orientation, but what specific form this takes is still unclear.

There is much talk in human research about discovering the **gene** that determines sexuality. It may exist, but I have my doubts.

Why would the brain have developed a gene that could potentially harm the continuation of the species? And if a sex gene is the answer, would it be a separate type of gene or perhaps abnormalities in the "sex gene" that accounted for each variety of sexual orientation?

The whole subject is all extremely difficult and I fear this discussion resembles a research paper that throws all the variables up in the air and is bound to end, *"More research on the subject is necessary."*

At the same time, one must accept that homosexual acts can take place between heterosexual animals that is not due to homosexuality. For instance, sexually active males, unable to obtain their own harem of females, may relieve their sexual needs with each other. That only shows that sexual urges need to be satisfied.

The *sex drive* itself is fuelled by hormonal and physical influences that develop up to sexual maturity. Slipping on a mantle of sexual orientation during this phase is the defining moment.

It is not that the animals are concerned what the outcome is. If they do find the same sex attractive, their community and whichever environment they find themselves in does not require a "coming out" declaration. How civilised.

So, the animal is sexually primed (biologically) and mentally stable (sexually), so the act takes place with the object of choice.

Despite considerable research on animal sexual behaviour, there has been considerably little on evaluating the factors influencing their sexuality. In the past, there have been such pearls of wisdom on homosexuality as, *"It must be due to a serious chemical imbalance in their biological make up."*

The statement that "Sexual orientation refers to the gender (male or female) to which one is *attracted*," for me remains the simplest and best description. All we have to evaluate now is what constitutes "attraction"?

It is definitely not a physical condition. It must be an inherited, *mental* condition (which I have already stated is not an instinct because it is not common to the species as a whole).

Is it a random condition, like blood types? (Different species can have a wide range of blood types). They are inherited.

If attraction is the result of a mental activity, and we know that animals are susceptible to inheriting *"memories,"*, could it be that animals *inherit the image of what they find attractive*?

They are predisposed to being attracted to animals of the same gender or the opposite gender, or both.

This may not be a scientifically proven fact, but then there are no scientifically researched facts to prove I am wrong. Sometimes, one just has to use common sense to reach a conclusion.

Another aspect of the importance of mental image in determining sexuality is the existence of *transgenders* in the animal kingdom. (A transgender is an animal with the body of one gender, but the mind of the other gender.)

There have been reports of hens that try to crow like cockerels or, having behaved normally as an egg layer, gradually undergo a natural sex change in that they grow flamboyant coxcombs, expansive tail feathers, and begin crowing. In terms of sexual orientation, it does not get any stranger than that.

No doubt, experts will come up with an explanation as to the mechanics of it, or claim they are merely April Fool stories.

I was more interested in what, if anything, such a "hen" was *thinking* during its life. Did it always wish it were a cockerel? Did it ever feel it was a cockerel in a hen's body? If the mind was demanding a sex change, and then achieved it, the body was in tune with the procedure and the result was a very contented hen/cockerel. If only we could know for sure. If only that hen could tell us how it had felt until it changed!

In the animal kingdom, it can confidently be claimed that *"There is nothing so natural as sexuality."*

Environmental Influences

Environmental influences have, I believe, less impact on animal behaviour than on humans. Their lives tend to be of a fixed routine in locations known to them and with recognisable dangers to be faced. Successful species can evolve and flourish comfortably for millions of years.

The environment has to be a friend, but when it no longer is, behaviour changes are required, either with annual migrations or enforced change of territory. In certain instances, where the habitat of a species is destroyed, the effects can be catastrophic if the species is unable to adapt or relocate to other acceptable regions.

Predators have always been the bane of animals. Meat eaters kill to survive, so meat sources from small to large form part of a food chain. No meat goes to waste in the wild, where survival is a constant battle. Non-meat eaters have often evolved with size, speed, or agility as their defence against predators.

The greatest catastrophe for animals, certainly the edible species, has been the emergence of Man. Only the smallest species on land have not been deliberately attacked by humans, unless they were deemed "nuisances." But anything that could be killed and eaten by humans has suffered, often to extinction or close to it.

Man has also removed the natural habitats of many species by the destruction of forests, removal of hedge rows, the use of pesticides, and over-fishing. Never before has the natural kingdom been under such attack by a single species. On land, in the air, or the sea, Man has taken a toll.

Yet it could be argued that Man has helped certain species by domesticating them. Animal farming has created a partnership between Man and beasts enabling both to co-exist, although use of the term "partnership" is ironic since it involves one partner rearing and then eating the other.

While some find this system offensive, others defend it as being necessary. Humans have always been meat eaters. Instead of annihilating certain species, they have domesticated them, thus enabling them to thrive and survive, usually without the constant threat of predators.

Unfortunately, we are unable to ask a sheep whether it would prefer to live and have lambs each year, or not to live at all.

Male animals fare worst in this arrangement. Where the domesticated animal is a food source, the females are valued for such things as their milk, their skins, or producing offspring. Most males are fattened and made ready for market as quickly as possible.

Even the relatively few prize males retained for mating purposes are in danger as modern means of fertilising the animals comes into vogue as more reliable and controllable.

Campaigners against the rearing and killing of animals for human consumption face an uphill battle because humans have always been a meat-eating species. If domestic cattle, sheep, pigs, and goats could not be reared as food, they would have become hunted into extinction. All land would be used for raising crops. If the animals had a vote in the matter, the choice would be between *"live and be eaten or become extinct,"*

The major environmental stress factor of most species must be that of avoiding predators. And the greatest predator has proved to be Man. Whether for meat, skins, horns, ivory, antlers, or sport, *Homo sapiens* is the modern, environmental predator and destroyer.

Even so, species that have survived Man's presence have retained their individuality.

PART TWO – HUMAN BEHAVIOUR

Having examined a number of factors influencing the behaviour of animals, we now turn to the latest species to climb the evolutionary tree—*Homo sapiens*

Homo Sapiens

Humans have evolved as the most complex species on the planet. They have become so dominant that, in their (comparatively) short time on earth, they have achieved control of the land, sea, and air, confident in the knowledge that any dangers to mankind will eventually be controlled and eradicated. What made us so all-conquering?

We reached this position of authority by virtue of having larger brains that enabled us to be cleverer, more innovative, and more destructive than all those that went before us.

Our species seems to have an insatiable desire to prove how far it can go—to compete until there is nothing left to achieve, and to go to the ends of the earth to prove our invincibility, even if it means destroying ourselves in the process.

This monumental achievement has come about by individual humans making personal contributions to the species, just as countless billions of individual social insects have contributed to their social communities for hundreds of millions of years. The difference between the two social systems is that the principal objective of the insects has always been *"survival and harmony within their environment."* Humans rapidly advanced far beyond such basic, simplistic goals.

What makes us so different? How are we evolving as a species and as individuals? Do we understand what we are trying to do with our existence? Have we even begun to understand ourselves, and which factors have really influenced our behaviour?

If we compare our abilities to those of other species, there is no comparison. Our potential, as a species, is incredible. Our potential as individuals is equally amazing. Our range of emotions, our ability to be kind or cruel, our mental skills, and our ability to innovate are all breathtaking.

We are still evolving as a species. We are developing physically and numerically because we have a better understanding of our bodies and their requirements. We are able to control the effects of major diseases, we have vastly improved food-producing methods, and we live longer. There is general agreement that the physical welfare of the species has a bright future, but there is no similar agreement when attempting to explain our mental and behavioural status.

Despite our incredible scientific, technical, and medical progress, there is still no unanimity as to which factors most influence our behaviour.

There is no apparent urgency by governments, professionals, or the public to promote greater understanding of human behaviour or to encourage greater awareness of the problems of mental health. Why not? Because the mental health professionals are not doing it, and the public is not demanding it.

Homo sapiens took control of their physical well-being during the last century. Now is the era to achieve similar progress in mental health welfare. Destructive forces explode in all parts of the world and, at home, we become more and more concerned on so many fronts about the younger generation.

To combat any feelings of helplessness, we must arm

ourselves with greater understanding of the problem areas and means of dealing with them. If we, the public, can come to understand more about behaviour, we will be better equipped to become involved in helping ourselves and the young of the future. How do we start?

For example, there could be a more pro-active approach on two fronts:

(1) The two major schools of thought on behavioural influences should be less combative and more cooperative.

(2) All theories regarding behaviour and mental health disorders, whether scientifically validated or not, should be deemed worthy of investigation until both "schools" reject them.

The main objective of any such processes would be to determine an agreed upon approach by the professionals to explaining behaviour and mental health issues. They need to put their heads above the parapet and declare where they stand on these issues, and then confidently set out to educate the public and the government.

"Awareness and prevention are always better than a cure."

Why is this necessary?

If that pro-active approach is achievable, it could lead to evolutionary strides forward in our mental well-being. We might even gain the ability to behave more responsibly.

All the major problems on our planet are man-made. We hate, we fight, we kill, and we destroy, as we always have done. Even worse, now it is predominantly against our own kind. No other species ever evolved to behave in such a manner.

On the other hand, no other species has possessed such depths of caring and compassion for the despair of others or the welfare of animals.

Our minds are so complex, yet no one helps us to understand why. We can only benefit from a different approach.

Can we play a part in this?

I think we can. This long-standing debate about hereditary and environmental influences should not remain just an intellectual argument between the professionals. It deals with matters that directly concern you and me. If we were to try to understand some of the issues and want to learn more, that would provide greater incentive for the professionals to help us. They need our support as much as we need theirs.

We could well end up having a clearer picture of who we are, and it could influence how we analyse and assess ourselves and our behaviour. We might even answer some of those questions lingering at the back of our minds when we read about *"the spectrum of Man's humanity and inhumanity."* We would develop the confidence to make a better job of assisting our children in the difficult task of growing up and their personal development, and confidence is precisely what we need and what the professionals can give us.

However, to attain such a "state of wisdom," we must first want to learn more about the issues. *Homo sapiens* has come to terms with understanding his body in the last century, and now is the time for coming to terms with his mind. But it must be done in the right spirit of searching for answers. Cast off the shackles of reticence, embrace the honesty of searching, abandon unnecessary professional rivalry, and tolerate the mistaken ideas of those who mean well.

I have to confess I have always leaned towards the **Nature** side of the argument because I am still influenced by memories of the rampant differences in the boys of our family. I never could accept that the qualities of my four bothers and me, either as individuals or as human beings, originated just from "life's circumstances."

There was something special inside each of us that made me want to seek out what it was. I then became fascinated with *Homo sapiens* as a species and was delighted whenever I felt I had found an answer to something puzzling me. I am one of those who grew up with and was inspired by David Attenborough's many magical television series on the animal kingdom because his programmes always made me think more deeply about our own species.

We are the latest major arrival on earth's tree of life. Evolutionary processes are a fact of life. Scientists can clearly demonstrate the evolutionary development of the human body and would love to find the so-called *Missing Link* to complete the sequence. They acknowledge the debt we owe to the past.

It seems to me that, in explaining the development of the human brain and mind, scientists have been unwilling to acknowledge any meaningful debt to earlier species. It is quite the opposite, in fact. They are reluctant to acknowledge that qualities essential to more primitive species could be present in the human mind. It is almost as if they had believed that aliens had plopped bodies on the earth's surface and said, *"Develop into a new species, so they faced the environment, and they encountered the traumas of living and, lo and behold, they evolved as the human species."*

That last paragraph is childish and petty, but it exemplifies my real frustration at the seeming inability of some professionals to accept that items that cannot be measured and proven scientifically might exist. It must really gall them that salmon cross thousands of miles of ocean to spawn in the rivers they came from, and the human brain is unable to explain how they do it. Describe it, yes. Explain it, no.

I am willing to believe that environmental factors seriously affect the mental state of people, especially if they are totally unprepared for them. But I also believe that ignorance of the early symptoms of mental disorders is a contributory factor. Like cancer, early detection leads to the most effective treatment. This should be a priority. Public education on mental health matters should be the primary goal for improving the mental development of our species.

There should be more public discussion and media attention given to the brain, the mind, and behaviour, what the pluses and minuses are, and what accounts for them.

There should be collaboration and commitment in seeking a consensus on the origins of human behaviour. By that, I mean one that can be presented to the public either in debate or as an accepted theory.

I am simply advocating positive action to enable ordinary people to become interested and involved in such activities. If that begins, then we might be inclined to feel that the mental future of the species could also be in good hands.

This book, despite its limitations, is offered as a contribution to a much needed honest and open debate on the subject, *"Which contributes most to human behaviour, Genetic Inheritance or Environmental Influences?"*

The Nature (Hereditary) Argument

Those supporting the Nature side of the argument do not accept that environmental influences dominate the process of personal development. They do not accept that one's personal development is an environmental "cause and effect" process. Besides, the spectrum of human behaviour is so varied that life's experiences would be incapable of creating so many *unique* people.

Those who claim the hereditary side of our nature is more influential in our development do not accept that we are "empty vessels" at birth who have to wait for life's experiences to enable us to develop personal qualities, such as character, temperament, and personality. They believe that, just as our physical appearance is endowed to us by our forebears, whatever exists in our brain at birth is also an essential part of our genetic inheritance. Otherwise, our society would be mainly divided into **bad** people (who come from broken homes living in slums) and **good** people (from loving families living in better quality accommodation.) Life was never that simple.

We inherit a ***genetic core of personal qualities*** that, in the same way as physical characteristics, is an amalgam or concoction of qualities randomly provided by our ancestral line.

Our DNA and gene pool went through the same process. That is why we are "unique." Siblings may have the same ancestral line, but they do not receive the same ancestral package, hence our differences, even under the same environmental circumstances.

Take the common experience of early rejection. Two boys pluck up courage and, for the first time, ask girls to go out on a date. They both get the slow head to toe examination and then are coldly told to *"Get lost."*

Boy A is mortified and embarrassed and vows it will be a long time before he gives another girl the power to humiliate him.

Boy B looks her up and down and quick as a flash quips, *"Thank God for that"* and walks off as if unconcerned.

The environmentalist would claim that **Boy A's** reaction was a perfect example of how life's experiences impact on a person's emotional development. Of course they do. It is as obvious as saying, "A person standing in the rain gets wet." But do they then say that the response of **Boy B** is also a perfect example. They both experienced rejection, but coped with it in their own way.

Had **Boy A** been better prepared before handing the girl an emotional whip, rejection would not have affected him so badly. The real cause of his hurt was not just his sensitivity. It was also his lack of preparedness for rejection. **Boy B** obviously had prepared a punch line in case he was turned down and, having delivered it, might even have walked away with a smile on his face.

If we inherit a genetic package, does that mean we are born *good* or *bad, strong or weak,* and not have any say in the matter? It's a good question. Receiving genetic inheritance from forebears begs the question, **"How far back do the forebears go?"** Well, of course, we don't know. Geneticists will no doubt answer that one later, but let us assume it goes back as far as your great grandparents. That would mean potentially you could receive "qualities or influences" from **two** parents, **four** grandparents and **eight** great grandparents—a total of **fourteen** forebears. If it went back a further generation, the total would be **thirty**!

The *genetic core* you receive would consist of contributions from any or all of them and remember, **the gender of half of the contributors would be opposite to your own!**

Let us assume these multifarious qualities or traits being assembled in your particular genetic line broke down into the good, the average, and the bad, and you will receive a random selection. Now the question is, *"What will I get?"*

Mathematicians would say that, in random selection, a small percentage would inherit more than their fair share of good qualities, and a similar percentage would have more than the average share of bad qualities. The majority of recipients would lie in between those two extremes and have a range of **plus** qualities and **negative** qualities.

That is not exactly a scientific explanation but, hopefully, it will enable the layperson to understand the point I am making about the randomness of genetic inheritance.

It is highly likely that our different individual reactions to situations, especially those experienced for the first time, are a reflection of our individual mental strengths or weaknesses or our temperament and other personal qualities.

A believer in genetic inheritance might claim that the reactions of both boys were perfectly normal. *Boy A* was just emotionally less able to deal with the situation than *Boy B*. As I said, had both of them been *prepared* for the ordeal of asking someone out on a first date, the reaction to rejection would have been less hurtful. Innate shyness can be overcome. If you have a personal "quality" you wish was different, you have to acknowledge that you need to deal with it, and then take positive steps to strengthen or improve it.

Let us consider families of four or more children. For the most part, they would experience the same family environment, certainly in their early, formative years. Some variables might include the differences from being the first or last born, being male or female, and their sexual orientations.

Could those of you who came from large families assess the differing characters, temperaments, and personalities of your siblings? Would you be able to begin to explain all or some of them? I never could when I was young.

This is why I believe the whole subject of what elements of life contribute to the making of a human mind and the behaviour that derives from it should be of interest to each and every one of us.

If the environmentalists are right in claiming that *"Experiences maketh the person,"* then the society we live in has a great deal to answer for.

On the other hand, if an essential part of our mental make-up could be shown to be inherited, we should try to embrace that fact. We should want to know to what extent these influences affect us. Can we promote "the positive" and counteract "the negative"? If we believed we could do that, we might be more willing to learn more about ourselves, as well as our fellow human beings.

Imagine a situation where you sit around a table with a number of people whom you know well and you all write down an honest assessment of the personal qualities (strengths and weaknesses, as they see them) of every one there, including yourself. Then, you each take away all the assessment sheets on you and compare their comments with the details on the sheet you wrote about yourself.

Would you do it? It could be so embarrassing and it might end friendships, but it would be revealing and informative if it could be done objectively.

That is what each of us needs at least once in our life if we are ever to discover who we are. Because who we are is not just who we think we are. We have to accept that we may be a number of "other persons" perceived by others.

For example, Scrooge benefited from being told about his public image and was able to change for the better.

If genetic inheritance is a major influence in our development, it can almost be guaranteed scientifically that most of us will receive both positive and negative qualities. We would definitely benefit if a process could be devised where we learn what others think of us. We have to try to determine what we can do to promote the positives and do something about the negatives.

I remember in my final school report before taking "A" levels, the English teacher wrote, *"If Bernard works really hard between now and the exam, he may obtain a pass."*

He had never inspired me as a teacher and it was obvious he did not think much of me as a student. Nevertheless, I needed success in that subject to get to university. Fortunately, his comments inspired me to devise my own approach to the exam, and I worked hard at it. When the results came out, I received top marks and the English Prize. I enjoyed that. (I later heard that the teacher declared he had lost all faith in the examination system). Honestly given criticism can be beneficial. Being unable to accept it is another personal flaw that needs to be addressed. No one said it was going to be easy getting to understand yourself.

We need to examine more aspects of human life to guide us towards one side or other of the Nurture versus Nature Debate.

You can see that our physical improvement as a species has served us well. This book endeavours to look for ways of understanding the origins of our mental behaviour because, if we can achieve that, it will help us to understand ourselves, and it may even lead to a better understanding of the origins of some of our mental problems.

Do Humans Inherit Instincts?

"Humans have no need of instincts."

This seems to be a commonly held view. After all, we are told that more primitive animals needed instinctive knowledge and skills to improve their chances of surviving in a hostile environment, and that *instinctive behaviour* is compulsive and unthinking.

"Humans do not have any need for compulsive and unthinking behaviour". We may be born helpless, but we are cared for. We acquire skills as we mature that enable us to survive in our working world. *"Who needs instincts when we have the State to look after us?"*

We learn in school that animal species would not have survived without their gift of instinct. It is understandable why people can reject any possibility of humans failing to survive without them. We have proved to be a self-sufficient species.

We may speak of maternal *instinct*, but we really mean maternal *feelings*. When we talk of an *instinctive* reaction, we really mean an *immediate* one. We often use the word, but we don't really mean it in its true sense.

Even so, we must not let ourselves be mesmerised or misled by the concept of "instinct." Although some of them do have mystical qualities, if we describe them in basic terms, they are merely *"Inherited information that influences behaviour."* So, instead of asking whether humans inherit "instincts," we should be thinking more along the lines of, *"Do humans **inherit** anything that influences their behaviour?"*

Assessing whether or not we *inherit* (genetically transfer) any behavioural influences is one of the aims of our journey. If we discover it is possible, then we must try to determine what they might be and whether they control us or we can control them.

If we think back to what was written in earlier chapters on the animal kingdom, it was claimed that genetic transfer included the exciting transfer of knowledge that led to skills, and other memories that assisted migrations and compulsive migratory behaviour. Also included was the transfer of many personal qualities, be they qualities of leadership, character, nature, or sexual orientation, or the *Cuckoo*'s non-maternalistic attitude to their progeny, and the *Robin* not fearing humans in the garden.

I also described **instinct** as the *genetic transmission of memories* because the source of a genetically transferred skill or knowledge is the memory bank of the originator.

This capability has continued in the animal kingdom for hundreds of millions of years. The question we should be asking ourselves is, **"Did it all stop when *Homo sapiens* came onto the scene or did the evolutionary process continue to include genetic transfer of memories in our species?"**

There is also doubt in my mind as to the validity of the view that instincts are essential for the survival of a species. I lean towards the view that instinctive behaviour evolves in successful species and can even be altered, as in the case of the *European Cuckoo*, which had to become a brood parasite to ensure its survival. Besides, so many examples of so-called instinctive behaviour have nothing at all to do with survival.

If that is the case, we are a young species and we might even be in the process of developing our own "human instincts."

"**Instinct**" is used to describe the *genetic transfer of knowledge and personal abilities that are accessed in an intuitive and natural way by successive generations.*

But most animal species inherit more than instinctive behaviour. Those that possess character, temperament, and personality are also born with their individual "personal qualities." Being of the same species does not mean being a clone. How do we know that? Because anyone associated with animals, domesticated or wild, knows they are individuals who do not **choose or manufacture** their personal qualities. Oh, their behaviour might be affected by environmental influences (e.g., humans), but their individuality is there from the beginning.

When did personal qualities arrive in the evolutionary process? When did personal qualities become a significant factor in a new species? We know that dogs and horses have them. How far back must we go? I am even inclined to believe social insects must have them to co-exist harmoniously with millions of others in a confined space, and they have survived a long time.

At this point, we need to remind ourselves that *"All instincts are inherited, but not all that is inherited need be an instinct."*

There is abundant evidence in the animal kingdom of individual personal qualities in a species being genetically transferred. Indeed the effectiveness of such genetic transfer has been the basis on which selective breeding has flourished for centuries. Animals with gentle or fierce temperaments have been selected to develop breeds specialising in such "temperaments." Prolonged breeding in this manner will develop a breed that has "instinctive" behaviour prevalent in that breed. Breeding has also concentrated on specific working skills for which certain breeds are famous.

So, we can rest assured that such skills can be developed and then genetically transferred to progeny. Eventually, certain behaviour will undoubtedly be described as inherited because they did not have to choose or earn those qualities. Every animal, pedigree, or mongrel has inherited personal qualities.

Transfer this to a human situation and we could speculate that men from the mountains of Afghanistan and Nepal would have an innate ability to be excellent fighters, whereas men in an Amish community would not. If that situation continued for thousands of years, then the mountain people would "instinctively" be warriors and the Amish pacifists.

Does that mean that a family that has farmed for generations will have descendants with the *inclination* to farm, or merely the *opportunity*? It's worth thinking about. After all, we do have the expression, "It's in the blood."

Are these conclusions about animals of any relevance when explaining human behaviour? Dare we consider them as steppingstones for understanding certain aspects of our own behaviour? I prefer a different question: *"Dare we not consider them?"*

This leads me to the inevitable conclusion that some, if not all, of our individual character and temperament are strongly influenced by our ancestry. If a particular quality could be repeated over many generations, then that quality would, over time, become prominent in that ancestral line. That would not mean because both parents are lovable people their children will also be lovable. However, it would improve the possibility if there were plenty of "lovable" people in the family line.

Fear is an ever-present emotion for animals because most of them are part of the food chain. Man has evolved as a natural predator, yet the Robin, a sparrow-sized bird in our gardens, is not afraid of us. It fears cats and predatory birds, but not the common enemy, Man? It is quite the opposite in fact. It will hop between our legs gobbling insects and worms as we turn over the soil in our garden. Anyone with a garden will have witnessed and been amused by this behaviour, so it is definitely an inherited behaviour pattern. As the cuckoo is born without normal feelings of avian maternalism, so the robin has rejected the natural avian fear of humans.

This teaches us that it is possible to pass on the emotion of **fear** or **non-fear** in an inheritance package. This is completely different from passing on **knowledge** of how to migrate for three thousand miles. This involves selective transfer of emotional behaviour.

We could carry on listing emotional factors involved in the mental "mechanism." The process evidently exists for brains of smaller size and significance. Surely larger brains could accommodate as much and more. Some of us are over-emotional and some of us are far less emotionally inclined.

Are we really such an advanced species that we don't need to inherit *anything* from our forebears; that we can select and acquire whatever quality and skills we need as we mature? Dare we tread the path of assuming we do not inherit anything useful? If this were to be the case, we need to be really convinced of it. We either gain nothing from our heritage, or it is an essential part of our existence and should be recognised as such.

Is it so difficult to accept the possibility that our personal ancestors, with an identifiable breeding lineage, could have contributed to an identifiable ancestral package that has some influence on us and all of our line?

If lower order animals can pass on species' instincts and personal attributes, can our species do less?

Is it impossible to believe that our brains, which have been nurtured in the womb for nearly nine months, possess the knowledge of fears or non-fears? Medical advice to pregnant women includes such tips as playing soothing music and not being emotionally distressed during pregnancy. Does this suggest that the mind of the unborn is an empty vessel that cannot be influenced?

Is it not within the bounds of reason to accept that personal qualities like application, ambition, determination, honesty, compassion, and humanity could be part of our heritage? Could we be born with leadership qualities, be one of those bound to be a follower or, worst of all, be one of those easily led into accepting the will of others?

Do you consider it might be possible to inherit a cornucopia of personal qualities garnered from our ancestors? We might even be "predisposed" to think or behave in certain ways and our environmental experiences are merely beating at the chambers of our latent inclinations.

If we inherit anything genetically, it is in the body and the mind. If our body is accepted as the sum total of our lineage, why reject **without proof** that the mind might also be influenced by our lineage? It is not as some believe: *"The mind is like a blank slate at birth, waiting to receive the writings of life's experiences."*

If we do inherit personal qualities and you discover your sibling is gentle, kind, and forgiving, while you are a loathsome specimen of humanity, what could you do about it? Well, for a start, if you are dragged into court for doing something terrible, you could always blame your *"ancestral package."* They won't have heard that one before and it sounds a more intelligent reason than, "I come from a slum."

I do not support the "blank slate" brigade. If I did, I would never have had the reaction I did to seeing the spider building its web, or when I first heard of the Monarch butterfly's epic journey. I would never have been dissatisfied when hearing the word *instinct* glibly used to explain bewildering animal behaviour.

Despite all I have read, nothing has yet dissuaded me from believing that the *"person we are at birth"* forms the lasting core of *"the person we become,"*, in spite of society's relentless efforts to mould us into the image it would like us to have. As individuals, we are not born as a vacuum, but as diamonds. We may be born with rough edges, and we may contain flaws and blemishes, but no matter how much smoothing and polishing the environmental influences achieve, diamonds we remain.

Let the **Nature vs. Nurture Debate** be heard loud and clear.

The Nurture (Environmental) Argument

Having explained that there is a fervent environmentalist lobby, we should try to understand their viewpoint more clearly.

It is easy to appreciate why advocates of the *Nurture Lobby* (the environmentalists) are so convinced they are right. They do not categorically deny the existence of some hereditary factors, but they believe life presents a long list of external influences on us, starting from our time in the cot and never ending until we are laid to rest in our coffins: family, home, friends, school, university, work, armed forces, church, local council, government, spouses, children, neighbours, the media, and so on.

So many external influences and most of them telling us *where* we should be, *what* we should be thinking, *why* and *how* we should be doing it, are all trying to mould us into the perfect child, teenager, employee, spouse, and citizen. How do we manage to cope with so many external pressures?

I would suggest that there are so many negative situations facing us during our lifetime, be they physical and sexual abuse or the many other stresses of surviving in a modern society, that numerous people suffer mental trauma. These external influences become identifiable as leading to mental stress and breakdown, which, of course, they are. If the traumatic situations had not been encountered, the serious mental issues may never have arisen. Consequently, the environmental conclusion is reached that life's experiences strongly influence who we are and what we do.

The other side of the coin is that we tend to react in a variety of individual ways. Some of us are compliant and are willing to *"go with the flow"* (anything for a quiet life). Others will be less malleable and may inwardly resent being expected to behave in a particular way. Then there will those who oppose being bossed around by anyone at any time in their lives and will make everyone aware of it. Finally, we have the deliberately disruptive element.

We all fit into or somewhere between those categories. Why are we so different? Why, as a species, are we not all compliant or aggressive? Even those raised in a similar environment will display vastly differing behavioural responses to the world in which they live. Some will be leaders, others followers. Some will be positive, others negative.

During the days of National Service, I underwent basic training in an army camp. After a fortnight, a number of recruits were chosen for officer selection training and moved to a different part of the camp.

We arrived on Friday afternoon and, from first stepping into the barrack room until Sunday evening, we were pushed around and shouted at as we were forced to bring our kit (uniform, boots, belts, etc.) up to the "required standard." We were quick-marched to meals, given fifteen minutes to eat, and then quick-marched back. Our kit was regularly inspected and thrown about because it was "never satisfactory," and lights out only occurred when we were exhausted.

Some recruits complained and said they *"Could not take any more."* They were allowed "to leave."

Late Sunday night, we were lined up (once again) to be told our "oppressors" were, in fact, recruits ahead of us who had volunteered to work us over for the weekend (while all permanent staff were mysteriously away), in order to get our kit looking immaculate before the official training began.

This story has a point to it. All recruits chosen for officer selection had been to university or had advanced educational qualifications. Most of us came from comfortable upbringings, yet individual reactions to the weekend's activities ranged from tears to good-humoured acceptance.

It demonstrates that we possess different threshold levels for application, determination, humiliation, and acceptance of the shock tactics thrown at us. I found that weekend really challenging. (On top of that, my kit looked immaculate come Monday!)

As I said earlier, environmental influences can have a powerful impact. Our fragile minds are tormented by pride, ambition, envy, guilt, frustration, hope, desire, disappointment, despair, and elation. No wonder mental problems remain the curse of our society. And the Nurture lobby wishes to take all the credit for it.

Ah, yes . . . The point of the Army example is that there are always two opposing forces involved when we have contact with an external influence: *what it is*, and *the way we deal with it*.

When someone from an unfortunate environment behaves badly, the temptation is to blame the environment. However, when someone from the same situation or locality does well and proves to be a role model for others, one does not hear the success attributed to the poor environment. The success is acknowledged as being achieved due to the qualities of the individual.

When people from a *privileged* background make a complete mess of their lives, the reaction tends to be close to bewilderment that such an environment could produce such devastating situations. I recall years ago when two brothers killed their rich parents to obtain their inheritance sooner. People found this unbelievable. I did not hear blame attributed to their upbringing.

I do not wish to go in any detail through a long list of external influences in our lives and try to prove whether or not they mould us, because we all know that they do affect us, in good and bad ways. We only have to look through our own lives and remember some special crossroads and the directions we decided to take; some special people we were lucky to meet at the right time; those we wished we had never listened to; the regrets we have at wrong decisions made and the smiles at the potential "disasters" we narrowly missed. And right in the middle of every incident was a decision-making process that we had to go through.

Did our "environment" encourage us to make the bad decisions, while we taught ourselves to make the good ones?

Early in life is when so many important attitudes and decisions are taken, in education and training, treatment of family members, and choice of friends and partners, but most of all in developing into the person we become: good or bad, reliable and trustworthy, or lazy and irresponsible. So many aspects of our being are waiting for our decisions. If we don't think about them and just let them happen, by the time we discover we made some wrong choices, it might be too late to change them. I think they call this phase "growing up." But that begs the question, *"When do we ever stop growing up?"*

The awkward process of being a teenager is when young people need help, whether they acknowledge it or not. Parents hear all kinds of stories about "teenager behaviour" and fear the worst. Not being a brilliant parent myself, I have to go back to my teens to recall what it was like. I cannot remember a single incident of "life guidance" from my parents, although I can recall a very effective "life lesson." But that's another story.

Adults need guidance on how to guide. There should be an accessible professionally produced template of helping young people to become more aware of life.

Many from wealthier backgrounds, despite their silver spoons, make poor personal life choices. Environment does not make the man, but it influences him.

You may be thinking I am now contradicting myself. I have been suggesting that much of who we are we are born with, yet I have suddenly switched to "making choices" as to who we will become, coming to "crossroads of choice." Why?

Just as I have claimed that animal behaviour is influenced by inherited factors, I have never accepted the argument that their behaviour is robotic. They are individuals within a species and provide a personal contribution to their behaviour (e.g., the lioness that fostered an orphaned deer).

I feel that humans are even more complicated with mental issues. Accordingly, their lineage reflects this. Few of us are born saints or psychopathic killers. Their paths must almost be chosen for them from day one. The rest of us are different. We are born with a lineage that includes the good, the bad, and the indifferent. Our brains contain a mixture of humanity that we have to deal with personally. Such a condition may predispose us one way or the other. Dealing with environmental influences is a personal battle throughout our lives. Battles require application and decisions. Otherwise, they become defeats.

Imagine a situation where the young could grow up in an environmentally friendly city. Discrimination and deprivation were eradicated and they were able to mature naturally without negative influences.

Would that city be a society of harmonious cooperation or would the individual nature of some citizens inevitably come to the fore and spoil it?

It is difficult enough coming to terms with the sort of person we find ourselves becoming, without the interference of society.

What gets me about environmental influences is that most of them are telling us what to do, how to behave, what to say, and what not to say. They want us to be respectful, hard-working, law-abiding, subservient, and harmless people who cause the state no problems.

After so many strong, threatening influences on our young minds, all encouraging, imploring, and insisting that we grow up to be respectful, responsible, law-abiding sons, daughters, students, employees, and citizens, how do so many of us still manage to make a mess of it?

Are we able to cope effectively with life or growing up? We could all benefit from better guidance or at least clearer guidelines as to how to cope with what life has to throw at us. Some are more fortunate than others, but for those requiring support with personal development or acquiring the skills of living, where is positive guidance to come from?

Parents: seem unable or reluctant to guide their children.

Schools: so occupied teaching facts that there is never the time in the curriculum for "teaching life."

Religion: teaching faith, not life.

Society: too busy looking after itself to help individuals.

Professionals in the field of human behaviour are without the opportunity or confidence to guide and help us cope with life's situations before they turn into mental problems.

Are you starting to form opinions of your own?

The Human Brain

It is amazing how most of us devote so little time to understanding the workings of our body. Biology was not in my school curriculum, and my family members never mentioned anything to do with the body. I guess it was the Age I was born into. Is it any better today?

We tend to become aware of important "parts" only when something is wrong with us or a close relative, and our first question is usually, **"What exactly *is a* . . . ?"** Then, we see what we can find out about it.

The brain is special. We need to consider it in some detail since it is going to be the focal point of all our topics connected with behaviour. Please take my word for it when I say it is the most complex item in the world (Let the scientists drive themselves crazy trying to fathom how it functions).

The *brain* is the physical matter contained within our skull that determines who we are and what we do. It determines our nature and our behaviour.

It breaks down into compartments with specific roles, and it possesses an incredible internal communication system. It also has areas that still baffle the specialists.

When I add that it has up to one hundred billion nerve ends (*neurons*) passing signals to each other via one thousand trillion connections making *neural* (nerve) *circuits* and pathways, you will understand why it is simpler just to accept that it is "complex and allegedly efficient."

I was interested to read that deep inside the human brain are remnants of the early reptilian and mammalian brains. So, we have biologically ancient parts of the brain, as in other parts of the body. That's a bit creepy, but is still a reminder of our evolutionary background.

The significance of our brain is that it determines who we are and how we behave. We are able to make some decisions as to how strong its influence is, but it is also more than capable of independently influencing what we do during our lives—so much so that, in examining what it does *for* and *to* us, I find myself asking: **"Is the human brain our servant or our master?"**

If you think that is a stupid question, I ask you to bear with me, as this thought will be developed when we look at certain individual topics.

Our dominance as a species is due to our brain's size and capability. It serves us well as we grapple our way through life's new experiences and challenges. It is life's tool for helping us to understand the world we live in.

There is one minor issue. It not only contains our conscious mind, it also encloses our *subconscious*.

We can all understand the role of our conscious mind. It is what we use when we are awake, active, and alert. It is what keeps us going during the day. We feel it is part of who we are. We endeavour to be, and believe we are, in control of it. It is the vehicle in which we travel through life.

Our *subconscious* is different. Few of us know anything

substantial about it, mainly because nobody bothers to tell us. And why are we not receiving any helpful information about an important aspect of our mental package? Because nobody can agree exactly what it is, where it is, and how it works, *and we don't bother to ask!*

One thing scientists almost unanimously agree upon is that it should not be called the *subconscious*, because that is not a "*scientific*" term. They feel it should be referred to as the **unconscious** mind, which means it is "not conscious." Well, I suppose that is a beginning.

I, on the other hand, shall continue to use the word *subconscious*, partly because I am not a scientist and shall therefore not be embarrassed to use it, but mainly because non-scientific readers recognise the word, whereas *unconscious* has other connotations for them. One comment on this subject I liked by someone was: *"There is more to being human than consciousness."*

And the more you read about the subconscious, the easier it is to become confused. Thinking about mind matters such as **memories, dreams,** and **mental disorders** pushed me further and further into trying to assess the involvement of the subconscious. One kept coming across comments like, *"The subconscious consists of thought processes that exist outside consciousness."*

And then there are statements indicating there is a long way to go before we understand the components of subconscious thought.

So, why do I carry on where better minds than mine are unwilling to tread? Because I am not trying to pinhole *how* the subconscious works. I want to express my misgivings about some of its functions and speculate as to which hereditary factors could be responsible.

Let me give you a couple of examples to illustrate what I mean.

Phobias

The anguish constantly experienced by someone with a phobia needs to be seen to be believed.

I am not talking about someone who was attacked by a dog as a child and has grown up with a great fear of dogs. A phobia is a compelling *dread* of a certain thing or a situation, and the sufferer often cannot explain the origin of the phobia.

A good friend of ours was terrified of spiders. I mean *terrified*. Their size did not matter since they all had the same effect on her. If she was home and a spider came through the patio doors, she would vacate the room or lift her legs up onto the sofa. If she watched the television, her eyes were constantly searching for "intruders." She was not able to kill them.

When my wife and I took her home after an evening out, our friend would stay in the car while I went through every room in the house declaring each to be free of spiders before she would enter her home. I knew her for over thirty years and her condition never changed.

When my wife became pregnant, I discovered she was absolutely terrified of cats. She told me she had never really liked cats, but her pregnancy brought this phobia to the surface with a vengeance. We were in Nicosia, Cyprus at the time, and wild cats were everywhere.

She insisted on hanging out the washing—but only when I was there to stand guard with a broom. We could not go to a party until I had rung up to check whether they had any cats. Once, the hosts begged us to go, insisting they would lock up the cat in a bedroom. My wife reluctantly agreed. During the party, a guest, looking for the bathroom, opened a bedroom door and the cat was out in a flash rushing across the floor. My wife saw it, and turned to escape over the balcony railing. Fortunately, someone grabbed her. We were on the twelfth floor! We never believed a cat owner after that.

When we retired, we lived in a villa with a lovely garden and swimming pool. In nine years, she went into the pool twice, and would not sit in the garden because she had seen neighbouring cats using our garden as a short cut. We eventually moved to a ninth floor apartment.

Her family could think of no incident with a cat when she was a child. It was just something she had to put up with.

Part of her terror is due to the fact that she is convinced that cats are *evil*. She says, **"They kill for pleasure,"** and her dread is that one will brush against her leg.

The effects of such phobias on sufferers are mainly long term. Reactions when faced by their "predator" become a conditioned response. That is a *consequence* of possessing a phobia. The source of the fear is not at the conscious level of the mind. It is deep-rooted. It is inaccessible. It feels as though it has been there "from the beginning."

Let me switch to another example of behaviour that is not as straightforward as it might appear.

A nasty piece of work

Some young people find it easier to become compulsive bullies, liars, thieves, disruptive influences, and generally nasty pieces of humanity.

I might accept environmentalists blaming their home life, their housing, their parents, their lack of self esteem, and all the other reasons were it not for the fact that other youths, with similar dispositions come from comfortable, middle and upper class families and have good educational opportunities.

Most young people, even when brought up in less than ideal circumstances, are not of this ilk.

Do anti-socially inclined youngsters consciously set out to acquire negative characteristics, or do they find themselves *becoming* someone who enjoys exercising power over weaker beings, enjoys inflicting fear and humiliation on others, or enjoys being acknowledged as a leader who is not only unafraid of authority, but is openly contemptuous of it?

Let us not forget that gender is not a factor. Girls can be as malevolent and merciless as boys.

I believe that some individuals have a predisposition to be confrontational. Social influences will have a part to play, if only to provide a protective stage for their activities but, for most, particularly the leaders, the impulse comes from within. They possess a driving force within them that they find hard to resist.

The *conscious* mind is not the depository for such coercion. The conscious mind is merely the vehicle for them. The conscious mind receives instructions as to how to behave; the subconscious mind frequently dictates what that behaviour will be.

This natural inclination to behave in a particular way need not be anti-social. Other young people are drawn into looking after injured animals, or wanting to be in the spotlight, or dreading having to speak in public. There are so many personal qualities that we would describe as *part of our nature.*

We must ask ourselves whether there could be a potentially controlling part of our brain that lies in a more secret, ancient, and mysterious place, capable of allowing even youngsters to torture and kill without experiencing a moment of remorse. *Evil thoughts.* If such a place exists in our minds, who programmes it? Which influences in our modern society created monstrous behaviour, or did environmental influences merely release it to a conscious level? So many questions.

Let us name such a location, the *subconscious*, "a place that can be in touch with the conscious mind, but is not necessarily part of it."

Whereas our conscious being is the person we think we are, we should be wondering whether our subconscious exerts far more influence on us than we or anyone else dare consider or admit.

Although the workings of the brain are essentially a mystery to us, we should attempt to consider some of its mysteries.

We can begin by examining three functions of the working mind:

Memories, Dreams, and Mental Illness.

The Mind – and Memories

Memory is the means by which the brain stores past sensations, experiences, thoughts, and knowledge. It is the sum total of everything retained by the mind. But, like all aspects of the brain, it is a massively complicated process, which even the scientists are still trying to unravel.

I mentioned in an earlier chapter the brain's process for storing and retrieving information, using *neurons* and neural circuitry. No matter what the "mechanics" are, we know that memories are not stored in one particular part of the brain. Different "types" are located in different areas, so it may be simpler for us to imagine the total storage system as being a *memory bank with separate chambers*. How they are stored and the specifics of retrieval are matters to be discussed and enjoyed by the scientists. We can benefit from trying to assess what our "memory bank" does for us, and try to enjoy some of its joys and complexities.

I have long been interested in the different levels and categories of memory. This interest was first aroused when I visited my hundred-year-old grandmother. She did not recognise me and thought my mother was the maid she had as a young girl. She lay in bed giving orders, as if she were still in the family home in Mold, North Wales. Her recent memory chamber was not capable of *recognising* her own child or grandchild, yet her long-term memory was functioning quite well. This final active part of her memory bank dealt with a different time zone.

How incredible at that age, when to all intent she was fairly ga-ga, her long-term memory was capable of retrieving ninety-year old events. I thought that was fascinating.

Since then I have had a special interest in the various "levels" of memory as I saw them because, even then, I felt if we did inherit anything mental, it was bound to be deeply entrenched in our *"memory vaults."* Purely for my own benefit, I began compartmentalising the memory bank into various *chambers*:

Immediate Recall Memories

This category is readily "retrievable." In my scientific innocence, I concluded that a retrieved memory (from whichever level) *"came to the surface"* of the brain and was active again. The most accessible would be recent experiences or those frequently recalled: what I had for breakfast, where I went last weekend, my wife's name, and famous sportsmen. And the memories didn't have to be recently installed. Ask anyone who enjoyed the experience of a special sporting event and they will immediately recall where they were, whom they were with, and even the names of the players.

Activity Memories

During our lifetime, we acquire numerous skills that can be work related, driving a vehicle, or playing golf or a musical instrument. Such things are acquired skills that we learn to do automatically and can employ them effortlessly at will.

What and When Memories

Then there are those memories you have to think a bit harder to recollect. What *was* his name? *When* did we buy this suite? These are things that happened some time ago and the brain needs time to retrieve them. These frequently are those bits of information you have not accessed often. It is interesting that, even when you have given up trying to remember, the brain will sometimes keep on working at it until suddenly the answer you were seeking comes to mind. This chamber becomes more active as you get older.

Trigger Memories

Then there are those forgotten ones that a taste, a smell, a song, or even a word can trigger the recall of people, places, or events decades before. "I haven't thought of that for years!" Such memories are hidden in another chamber requiring a separate key to open the door to release memories as clear as day (well, almost).

Recessed Memories

These are memories that are not readily available to the conscious mind and do not respond to normal methods used to retrieve other memories. For example, I have certain strong memories of my three-year evacuation to Wales during the War. During that period (aged six to nine), I must have acquired many memories that I am sure could only be brought to the surface now under hypnosis.

Long-term Memory

As I said, my grandmother's involuntary recall of her child-hood fascinated me. At the time all other memory chambers had collapsed, her *long-term* one functioned surprisingly well.

This was interesting because it clearly reveals that each type of memory could be located in its own part of the brain. Also, how revealing, and possibly significant, that the long-term memory chamber should be the most protected against the ravages of mental degeneration, even when a hundred years old.

Who would have thought that the functions of memories would be so multi-faceted, and all under the direction and control of the nebulous subconscious mind?

The subconscious also has the task of re-allocating the memories from chamber to chamber. What may be readily accessible today later becomes a *trigger* memory until eventually it ends up in the forgotten or long-term memory chamber, and it is our subconscious deciding when the time is right and transferring them accordingly.

Inevitably, this suggested to me that, if we did inherit *ancestral* memories of any kind, they would be similarly stored, secreted in some hidden chamber waiting to be accessed via a special mechanism, be it external or just another function of the subconscious.

No wonder the scientists are still trying to work out the mysteries of memory!

Dream Memories

This is one category we can accept because so many times during our lives, we wake up and shake our heads and wonder why on earth we were dreaming such a dream.

Our brain seems to have a mind of its own (no pun intended). We go to sleep and it is like going to the cinema. We experience incredible stories that include people, situations, fears, embarrassments, locations, and everything else all jumbled up.

The fact is that the brain deposits our experiences where it chooses and recalls them nightly as it pleases.

Cellular Memories?

This is a modern concept brought about as a result of transplant surgery. There is an increasing amount of anecdotal evidence claiming that a person who receives a transplant (heart, liver, kidneys, etc.) may experience a change in personality that appears to incorporate certain interests (love of classical music, sports, poetry, etc.) of the organ donor.

Is it possible that cellular matter other than the brain can contain memories? It seems unlikely, but where the mind is concerned, one can never say, "never." We are still almost in the Dark Ages of understanding the workings of the mind.

However, I find it hard to accept that any memories are deposited in the heart or other body parts even if there is anecdotal evidence saying otherwise. There you are! I am behaving like a scientist already.

Memories are activated in the brain. If scientists are to be believed, they are the products of interaction between nerve ends. When they are installed or recalled, they do not involve DNA. They are an example of the magical processes the mind is capable of. They are not physical items that can transfer to other parts of the body.

If DNA was a factor in the possession of memories, scientists would be checking newly born children to isolate any inherited "memory genes" or, later in life, identifying new memory genes.

Because memories are not physically identifiable, I don't see how it can be claimed that human memories *cannot be passed on* to the following generations. Once again, I refer to the numerous examples in the animal kingdom of doing precisely that.

Collective Memories

There is a train of philosophical thought that claims that we are all born with "collective" memory patterns. Just as a herd of animals will behave as one when some fear causes a stampede, so there is a *Homo sapiens* built-in collective response in given situations. For example, a crowd can quickly become a mob that turns into a rampaging mob, or a fire in a crowded disco that rapidly leads to panic and self-preserving desperation. It is a case of being swept up and led away collectively and irresponsibly. Some might say it is caused purely by fear, which is true. But the rapid transition from individual fear to crowd panic could well be an instinctive collective reaction.

Past-life Memories

This heading may come as another shock to some of you, but "past life regression" has a big following. It involves drawing on memories of so-called "previous lives" under deep hypnosis.

As you can imagine, believers in reincarnation consider past life "memories" as evidence supporting reincarnation as a reality. (See Chapter 25.)

The big question is, *"Could we each possess a chamber in our minds that contains ancestral memories passed on to us?"*

When I first came across this suggestion, my immediate response was to consider the idea seriously because by then I accepted the principle of inherited memories as being another description of instinct.

There have been amazing stories of people who have undergone hypnosis aimed at age regression to the point of recalling a past life. In some cases, the information revealed under hypnosis was of people centuries earlier, in foreign languages, and about locations that no longer exist, but later verified by experts.

Past life regression went through a popular phase and thousands underwent it. The sessions were conducted and recorded by reputable hypnotists under "controlled" conditions. The results have been rejected by the scientific community as flawed because, as with dreams, the process of recollecting memories is not reliable. "Such memories could well have been derived from historical novels, films, television programmes, general reading, and stored in the brain."

In the West, we live in societies that react suspiciously to a person who claims to have memories of past life experiences. To put it frankly, they are looked on as crackers.

Shirley Maclaine strongly believed one of her past lives had been as an Egyptian princess. You can imagine the press and public reaction to that statement! Glen Ford, the actor, revealed information under hypnosis about the exact position of the grave of some ancestor in a remote English village cemetery. Eighteenth century records did not reveal details of it, but further investigation eventually revealed there was an unmarked grave in the very spot Glen Ford suggested. He had a gravestone erected there.

Stories like that give a flavour of mystery to this type of memory. But, as scientists say, *"flavours are not proof."*

You should be aware that there are two ways of interpreting the description of "past (previous) life memories."

People accepting reincarnation as a fact of life believe the revelations under hypnosis are of the *individual's* previous lives. A second view is that such revelations are *ancestral* memories that come in the "ancestral package."

You might feel that both explanations are rather scary and hard to believe, which is precisely why scientists do not accept them.

I shall deal with this subject of past-life memories in more detail later (see chapter 26). I include it here solely to illustrate yet another possible, hidden chamber in our minds.

To those of you who have immediately dismissed this idea of "past lives" as ridiculous, I would ask that you do not rush into making up your minds.

Inherited Memories

Recent research has proved that some animals have a form of neural circuitry in the brain similar to humans, albeit on a much smaller scale.

With no other means of proving how insects *inter alia* genetically transfer intricate knowledge and urges to future generations, one must assume that it is accomplished by some method allied to neural circuitry.

Researchers will discover some form of micro neural circuitry in small insects. Otherwise, what explanation is there for the transfer of information needed for something like a three thousand-mile migration?

If we can accept that the genetic transfer of instincts is a fact and that instinct is inherited memory, it is not exactly a "giant leap for mankind" to say that **instincts are inherited memories.**

There will be other specialist categories of memories, but those we have above are sufficient for now. It is time to consider another aspect of the mind.

The Mind – and Dreaming

Dreams are a regular occurrence in our lives, but what purpose do they serve? Most people, given the choice, would prefer to do without them, yet are unable to stop them.

We are told that the content of many dreams can be linked to everyday activities and one's emotional state. It is even claimed that they are beneficial. People we might have known slightly decades before can suddenly play a starring role for us. Sometimes, the dreams are so bizarre or scary, we wonder, "Where the hell did that come from?"

Their content consists of images, sounds, and emotions. Anxiety is considered by some to be the most common emotion experienced, but there can be feelings of helplessness, abandonment, joy, and fear and, of course, sexual pleasure. Two out of three people are thought to experience recurring dreams.

It is said that while we sleep, the brain cannot simply close down for a rest period. Just as our physical organs carry on working while we sleep, the brain also remains surprisingly active. Although some "consciously active areas" regenerate while we sleep, there is considerable electrical activity in the brain, and our dreams are merely a result of that process. Some people even see dreams as a mental release mechanism.

It is not known for certain why and where dreams originate in the brain, but they are recognised as being a product of our subconscious mind. I use the word *subconscious* as meaning *"that part of the mind outside one's conscious awareness."*

During the day, with my conscious thoughts and actions, I consider myself to be in reasonable control. My mind deals with external information affecting me, and it responds readily to my constant flow of instructions. If I want to, I can spend time thinking about pleasant, frightening, sexual, or embarrassing situations I may have experienced in the past. This is sometimes referred to as daydreaming.

So, what is so different when, during sleeping hours, the "conscious me" relinquishes control? Does a *"subconscious me"* take charge until normal service is resumed when I awake?

Is this *"other person"* (or God forbid, other persons) in my head deciding to have fun, with hours of non-interference from "the sleeping one"? The dreams flow forth as if someone or something has adopted the mantle of "dream director," selecting a combination of neurons and then, via neural circuits, creating more nightly masterpieces.

Am I alone in being slightly uncomfortable with the fact that my mind initiates a nightly programme of mental activity we have come to call "dreaming"? Even more disturbing for me is the probability that these activities appear to be a "selective" rather than a random process.

What process, or which authority, plays with my neural circuits, memories, and emotions at night? I don't want it to happen, yet I cannot prevent it.

I can accept that, like the need for blood to continue flowing when I sleep, the mental energy and neural circuits are not shutting down, either. But there is an important difference between the two. Blood circulation, being a constant, physical function dependent on the beating of my heart, requires no mental input, whereas selective, mental activity (like dreams) does.

Dreams are not *random* interactions of electrical connections within the brain that have been triggered by recent experiences or hormonal conditions. Dreams frequently have themes, and *themes need to be selected, developed, and presented.*

The idea of an inner, mental me controlling these activities is not an unreasonable hypothesis. What could be wrong with that? Nothing, so long as it did not lead to future complications for me in my conscious state.

If our subconscious mind has the ability to control and manipulate thoughts and memories while we are asleep, does that not raise the possibility that, under certain circumstances, it **might also exert similar unwanted influence on our thoughts and behaviour when we are awake?**

We consciously *select* the subjects of our *daydreaming.* Even if we accept that some dreams are triggered by our thoughts or experiences during the day, this does not apply to surprising, weird, and frightening dreams. Which source in our sub-conscious inspires and selects those?

My concern about the *management* of my mind during my non-conscious state may stem from my ignorance of the actual mechanics of the neural circuits of the brain. But I do feel that the apparently non-random content of dreams requires a reassuring explanation from those who are knowledgeable on such matters.

These are interesting questions that I feel could be addressed by the professionals. To explain dreams simply as *"a beneficial mental release of subconscious thoughts, emotions, and fears"* is not a scientifically precise definition for me because it explains *what* is taking place and ignoring the *how.* There need to be clearer explanations on the sourcing of dreams and their selection. But most of all, we need to be thinking of the possible greater influence of the subconscious on our lives.

When one talks seriously of "losing one's mind," what is meant is, *"I am losing* control *of my conscious mind."* If that should really happen, which "mind" would then be in control?

It would be reassuring to learn about such mysteries of the mind, if only to reassure ourselves that they are natural and harmless, or to determine whether they could be instrumental in harming us.

If this conjecture about dreaming is considered overly dramatic, then someone should explain why it is. Just because the subconscious is a nebulous entity and difficult to describe does not preclude it from being more influential than we might think.

If these possibilities are unrealistic, it would do us no harm to be reassured of the fact. I am seeking logical reasons to explain my concerns over the mechanics of dreams. But when dreams include places I have not visited for years and people who are long dead, I cannot avoid feeling that some identity or control (call it what you will) is drawing mental threads together and is quite capable, night or day, of leading me in a merry dance.

And it is no use trying to reassure me that dreaming is a natural activity of the brain, or describing dreams as an innocent and healthy product of our subconscious.

We assume that the conscious mind is stronger than the subconscious when we are awake. What if that situation were reversed?

What happens if our subconscious has the ability to take control of our mind during our conscious hours?

The Mind – and the Subconscious 19

The last chapter centred around my thoughts on dreams, the process of their manufacture in our subconscious, and our apparent lack of control over them.

I want to develop further other possible influences and their ramifications of the subconscious in our lives. But first, I should explain further what I understand by the term **subconscious**.

One would think this would be easy. As non-scientific lay-persons, we can accept that our conscious mind functions when we are awake, and our *subconscious* functions when our conscious mind is no longer in control of our thoughts and deeds, (i.e., when we sleep).

Having accepted the possibility that our subconscious *takes over* when we sleep, we must ask ourselves exactly what we understand by that.

The state of being "in charge" implies direction and control. We feel that we are in charge during the day when we direct our mental and physical processes. One might even describe our input during waking hours as being the controlling *entity*. What form of "entity" could possibly be in control at night when conscious direction ends? Does it have a "mind" of its own which we can call our *subconscious mind*?

Is this "mind" merely nervous energy or electrical circuits in the brain continuing to work of their own accord, or is it still under some form of direction? I would not subscribe to any description of the subconscious mind as being engaged in "*random*" activity. If not random, what is a better description?

I am **legally** not responsible for what I say or any actions my body takes when I am not in a conscious state. Yet so much of my subconsciously-controlled night activity, including dreams, talking, and walking, seems to have a human influence. Can *someone* be in charge of my subconscious mind, or is there some other answer? The subconscious is more influential than our conscious because it is fully active twenty-four hours a day.

If you are beginning to think I am appearing paranoid about this, please be generous and bear with me.

When someone talks in their sleep, "who" is controlling the content? Night talking ranges from mumbling to intelligible statements. Apparently, the type of voice may even sound "different" from speech when awake. When the talkers awake, they remember nothing. It is as if "someone else" said it.

"Modern science and the law accept that sleep talking is not a product of the conscious mind and is therefore (usually) inadmissible in court."

It is no use scientists telling me that sleep talking, like dreaming, is merely the result of random interaction of neurons and circuits in a mind that cannot rest when we sleep.

Then, there is sleep walking. Although it usually occurs in children and they eventually grow out of it, a small percentage of adults continue to do it. Their eyes are open and they appear to be functioning normally. Some of them even travel considerable distances (as if in a conscious state).

It is not unknown for a person to commit homicide when asleep, and then be found not guilty of murder on the grounds that the act was *"not a product of the conscious mind."*

It might be thought that talking and walking in our sleep occur when our "subconscious" is closer to a state of consciousness, as when dreaming. But can that be true? Dreams can be remembered. The sleep talkers and walkers do not remember anything when awakened, so whatever the subconscious is, it is in charge of what we are doing when asleep.

Just as our conscious mind uses different parts of the brain to operate, so must our subconscious.

Why is learning more about our subconscious important?

You may be thinking I am getting overly excited or overly concerned about the role of the subconscious mind. You may feel that, so far as you know, there have been no alarm bells ringing on the subject, so there cannot be much to worry about. Perhaps you are right, but I still consider that there are possible disturbing implications about the influence of the subconscious. It is important to understand more because it can be a *dominating and controlling* force in our body. **It** is capable of making us dream, talk, move, and act, all without permission from us. **It** can make us smile, squirm, or sweat with fear whenever it wishes.

We like to think that our conscious mind *always* has absolute control of our thoughts and deeds during waking hours and that the subconscious always "willingly" gives way to that domination when we wake? Is that always the case? For example, when something triggers a very unpleasant, unwanted memory, does my conscious mind resurrect it (without any instruction on my part to do so) or has my subconscious mind decided of its own accord that it should be resurrected?

If the answer to that is *"We don't know"* or *"Further research is needed,"* we have a problem because it invites the inevitable question, **"Is the mind our servant in our conscious state, but our master when our subconscious takes control?"**

You might not be concerned about this control when you sleep. It is natural and there can be no harm in it. Everyone experiences it. When we wake, the conscious takes over and the balance is restored.

Would you be so relaxed if you thought this balance could be altered? What if our subconscious could dominate our conscious during waking hours? That would by scary. Why? Because we already know what it can do with our thoughts and memories when left to its own devices while we sleep.

Let us imagine a scenario where it does take over from the conscious mind during waking hours. What might happen?

Presumably, it would exercise its skills at producing situations, story lines, characters, emotions, fears, personalities, and whatever else it wanted from our memory banks. It would be playing games and, no doubt, we would end up feeling we were *"losing control of our mind."* The only escape from the "mind player" during the day would be unconsciousness or, more likely, medication and excessive alcohol to suppress it or blank it out.

Does our subconscious have compartments of activity?

The philosopher *Carl Jung* believed that the subconscious had two distinct compartments—the **collective** and the **personal**. The *collective* subconscious would contain mental qualities "common to the species *Homo sapiens.*" The *personal* subconscious would include events and emotions experienced during the person's lifetime that have found their way into the subconscious.

Perhaps we can explain this idea of the "collective and personal" more clearly by describing the *physical* attributes of the human body:

- my *collective* physical appearance makes me immediately identifiable as a member of the species *Homo sapiens*.
- my *personal* physical appearance will have been strongly influenced by the physical features inherited from *my* lineage (the colour of my skin, hair, and eyes or the shape of my body, nose, and ears, as well as fingerprints and DNA). They all combine to make me identifiable as an individual human being.

The collective subconscious might well include such basic reactions as "crowd hysteria" and primordial emotions like hate, anger, and self-preservation.

In our quest for knowledge of who we are and why we behave as we do, it is our *personal subconscious* that is important.

Why is the Personal Subconscious so important?

The personal subconscious is important because it is where our *individuality* lies. Just as we inherit the colour of our eyes and the shape of our ears from our ancestral line, so we inherit a multitude of neurons and circuits (or whatever constitutes our memories). We inherit a hotpot of potential personal attitudes, tendencies, vices, qualities of leading or following, predisposition to bravery or cowardice, unknown inner turmoil whether to be kind or cruel, what makes you see things as being attractive . . . and the list goes on.

The natural place for them to go initially would be our subconscious to be drawn upon as we grow.

Whichever personal qualities we inherit are a part of our individual make-up. That does not mean they will all necessarily surface to become a part of our individual persona. Without our knowing, many will. But some deeper facets of behaviour, both good and bad, may need to be nurtured or *triggered* into becoming part of our conscious character. When the Church or State authorises and encourages individuals to commit atrocities with impunity, there will be those who refuse to do so because it is not in their nature. But there will be others who discover that they are willing to answer the call. Then, there will be some who will wallow with pleasure at the sheer cruelty of what takes place. Such responses can only be already present in the subconscious.

How can I make such claims? What qualifies me to spout on about *the personal subconscious*?

I qualify on the grounds that I have one that has strongly influenced my development as a human being, and I know that because I never knowingly set out to give myself a particular temperament, or a certain character, or the personality I ended up with—just as I am certain my four brothers and three sisters did not knowingly create or manufacture theirs. External circumstances may influence who we become, but our multi-faceted package as unique human beings stems from within and exists in the subconscious.

Does that mean that we are *blessed or condemned* by our ancestors? No. I am not saying we are potato seeds who will never turn into apples. I am saying that the very essence of evolution, which includes a personal inheritance from our parents and ancestors, should make us aware that we have more say than we might think in becoming the person we wish to be.

How can we become involved in that process when we have never been taught more about our mental origins? Such knowledge could make us stronger when facing personal conflicts.

I believe that if the professionals could be persuaded to explore the existence of these latent personal qualities, they might well be able to play a greater role in our personal development.

Some people are lucky and discover they possess that *salmon-like urge* to do something special. It becomes a driving force that spurs them to express themselves in music, art, medicine, sport, or just to help others. Those of us who may possess such gifts that have not surfaced need to understand ourselves better to be able to search for incentives.

This may all sound rather vague at the moment, but maybe that is because you have not yet started the journey of finding yourself.

Are you the sort of person you want to be? Is your public persona one you are proud of? Have you made any conscious effort to develop additional personal qualities that you admire in others? Have you let things drift for far too long or have knowingly been influenced adversely by others?

First, you must believe that your personal subconscious contains so many qualities handed down to you that can be accessed. There is the saying that, *"You will never know whether you like it or are any good at it unless you try it."* If we have inherited qualities from our forebears, there must be many good ones amongst them.

We should all think and learn more about our subconscious because it is a most influential *entity* in determining who we are and how we behave.

It is claimed that the subconscious is different and separate from the conscious mind. But how inter-connected are they? For example, normally I sleep very well. When I have to get up earlier than usual for a golf match, I set the alarm. My sleep pattern that night tends to be more disturbed as I will frequently wake up to check the time. This indicates a connection between my subconscious and my conscious.

Bearing in mind its influence and potential power over us, should we be worried that it is located in such a fragile place—our mind?

If it intrudes of its own accord into our conscious, should we not be concerned?

The Mind – and Mental Disorders

There should be more open discussion on the subject of mental illnesses to promote awareness of early symptoms of the most common ones and greater sympathy for those experiencing them.

We know that **Dementia** and associated disorders are on the increase as a consequence of a much older population, but mental disorders can begin at a comparatively young age and, in many cases, last for life, with devastating effects.

The scientific community is still learning about the working of the human brain. They are also still trying to understand the numerous mental disorders and, if they are honest, they are still floundering to explain their causes with any real confidence.

Psychologists and research scientists tell us that the person we become is essentially the product of the countless external influences we encounter during our lifetime. The corollary of this is that most *"malfunctions of the mind must have been caused by traumatic life experiences."*

This emphasis on external influences being the major factor in our development has bewitched scientists into seeing life's distressing experiences, individually or in combinations, as the main cause of mental illnesses and that only through the objective clinical and scientific study and research will it be possible to understand them fully and develop proven methods of treatment.

Meanwhile, they employ therapeutic measures to give support to the patient by identifying and discussing the traumas that *"caused"* the mental illness. If the patient requires additional support outside of therapy, then medication is provided to suppress disturbing aspects of the illness. Should the patient reach the stage where the side effects from the medication are deemed to be worse than the disease they were suppressing, the therapist and the patient have a more serious problem.

Some illnesses run in families. The professionals accept that genetics (heredity) can also be a causal factor, hence their enthusiastic support of research into the role of DNA abnormalities being the cause of some specific mental disorders.

Despite more than a century of research, dedication, and arguing, they will be the first to admit there are **no known causes** of mental illness. There are *theories*—and the professionals are still arguing amongst themselves about those.

Should we accept their theories?

Life can throw up a range of disturbing experiences that can affect our emotional well-being and state of mind. It is easy to understand why the professionals would attach great significance to their impact on the relatively fragile human mind. They must have considered and rejected other possible causes. However, traumatic external experiences conveniently offer all the prerequisites for scientific study and research in that they can be identified, quantified, analysed, and discussed objectively with the patients.

Should we accept their theory as gospel? My view is that we are entitled to query some of their hypotheses.

Unfortunately, the professionals carry the burden of having studied the greats like Freud and Jung, spending years of study absorbing their theories in great detail. To reject or disagree with their heroes would almost be implying they were "better" than their mentors. Fortunately, I carry no such burden.

We all experience stressful situations. There are many shocks awaiting each of us on the journey of life. Some come at an early age, such as when millions of children were suddenly torn from their families during the Second World War, and some were moved around from house to house for years where their only apparent value (for some) was the financial benefits they brought with them. Countless others will have endured similar traumas from being orphaned, bullied, losing loved ones, or parents divorcing. Many of these and other dramatic childhood memories have stayed with us all our lives, but, somehow, most of us manage to deal with them and survive reasonably intact.

Adults face their fair share of "external influences," such as physical and sexual abuse, divorce, bereavement, failure, rejection, regret, and feelings of inadequacy and hopelessness, to mention but a few. Some people are pushed near the edge by such experiences whilst others learn to cope with them, often surprising themselves with their resilience

But quite a number are not so lucky. They prove to be more mentally fragile and react differently. They enter a frightening world where they are not fully in charge of their mind. We who have not been there cannot even begin to imagine the scale of their suffering. They deserve, and are entitled to, the best possible treatment.

I, without any professional training in psychology, could deduce that childhood sexual and physical abuse, dysfunctional family background, and a deprived childhood could dramatically affect a person's mental state and behaviour.

So much blame is given to various negative environmental influences, it makes me wonder how anyone who is well educated, not abused as a child, and has a comfortable family background living in a "good area" has the **audacity** to develop a mental disorder. What about depressed young men and women who have not had time to face traumatic experiences? What is their excuse?

Because the same myriad of so-called causes seems to be quoted whenever one researches a specific mental illness, I have selected one serious disorder to illustrate my concern at what I consider to be the current, blinkered approach to diagnosis and treatment.

Multiple Personality Disorder (MPD)

There are many personality disorders ranging from having violent mood swings to displaying multiple personalities. I would like to comment on one of them, *Multiple Personality Disorder* (MPD).

I will begin by listing some the considered symptoms and causes of the disorder.

Symptoms of MPD
- *multiple attitudes and identities that are not similar to each other*
- *can include flashbacks of abuse or severe traumas*
- *unexplainable phobias*
- *depressions*
- *loss of memory regarding other identities*

Causes of MPD
- *overwhelming stress situations or childhood abuse*

> – *traumatic memories and feelings that go into the sub-conscious and then emerge in the form of separate identities*
> – *repetition of stressful situations at different times helps to create different identities*

The diagnosis of MPD requires that two or more distinct entities or personalities regularly take control of a person's behaviour. Interestingly, there is memory loss involved where one "entity" has no memory of the others.

Although research indicates several areas of the brain that **may** be linked to this condition, it is admitted that there is "*no way to know for certain what causes MPD*. In fact, it is a little understood area of psychology."

The usual combination of traumas, particularly extreme stress and sexual abuse during childhood, are considered to be the main causes of the development of additional *identities* or *personalities*.

There is a school of thought in psychology that rejects the claim that a patient has *multiple personalities*. Their theory is that a person has only one true personality, which "splinters," revealing separate parts of that prime personality, before returning to make it whole again. The whole and the splintered personalities have no memory of each other. I should add that other professionals reject this theory.

My comments

It is surprising that, compared with so many dramatic advances in communications, weaponry, space flights, and medicine, understanding the mind appears to have remained practically immobile.

If I suffered from MPD, I would want to know what caused

it, but especially interested in knowing the *origins* of my additional personalities. Where did they come from? Such explanations as, *"traumatic memories and feelings go into the subconscious and emerge as identities,"* in all honesty, strike me as desperate, and unworthy of the profession. Environmentalists tell us our character, temperament, and personality are honed by our environment and life's experiences, then they tell an MPD sufferer that these "extra" identities are **caused** by severe abuse and other traumas suffered "when a child."

To me, displaying multiple personalities requires two causal processes. The first is the *creation* of the personalities and their placement in the subconscious; the second is the *trigger that activates them* into emerging in the conscious state.

An explanation such as, *"sexual abuse suffered in your childhood"* appears to be stating that the two separate processes, the **creation** *and* **emergence** of additional identities, are one and the same process. It is also suggested that repetition of the sexual abuse results in the creation of the further personalities as some form of escape mechanism from reality.

I would accept that traumas could trigger the *emergence* of additional identities, and might even agree that a single, additional identity could be the mental outcome of severe traumas. To add that they are responsible for the creation and emergence of additional personalities, some being strong, others weak, male and female, and even of different sexual orientations, is not nearly so credible. If each severe trauma created a new subconscious identity, by what mechanism does a single mind create such contrasting identities?

I would expect essential functions of the brain, with its neurons and neural circuitry, to receive information, collate and store it, and then retrieve as and when desired. I can even see how this process might prompt the mind to be happy or depressed, but creating new and separate identities calls for a creative ability. It involves independent decision making and invention, with no accredited input from the conscious mind. **What possible source could the subconscious tap into to create new and very separate identities?**

Is this diagnosis of inventive capability on the part of the subconscious explained by the professionals or merely proclaimed as the best explanation they can think of?

If traumas did not *create* them, it begs the question, *"How did the extra personalities come to be present in the subconscious?"* A sufferer does not knowingly manufacture them, and while I can believe that the effects of traumas become deposited in the subconscious, I fail to grasp that they would be capable of creating additional personalities with so many differences between them.

These personalities are sometimes referred to as *alter egos* (another self). It is you, but it is "another" you. Usually there is one more dominant than the others. (You can see where the *"splintering* of the personality" idea came from). I presume the splintering personality theory also came into being because it is more logical and has more scientific merit than the effects of violence emerging as multiple identities. However, that does not mean it is a better, workable theory. Some sufferers have been known to display up to a hundred personalities. How many splinters can there be?

Logic also leads me to assume that, if the subconscious and traumatic experiences do not **create** numerous new identities, and no other external causes are identifiable, then these identities must be of *internal* origin. They are present in the subconscious *before* the illness, and the external traumas are merely the catalyst for forcing them into the conscious state.

If MPD sufferers possess them before the traumatic experiences, then it has to be assumed that this phenomenon is a natural feature of the human brain. Therefore, *we must all be born with additional "identities" secreted in our subconscious.*

Think about it. If you (and the professionals) cannot think of a more reasonable explanation as to how multiple personalities come to exist **after** we are born, it stands to reason we should at least *consider* whether they were there **when** we are born. In other words, we inherit them from our forebears.

This theory about the origin of multiple personalities has far more credibility than claiming that traumas both create and activate them at the same time. If it could be **proved** scientifically that the subconscious is capable of naturally possessing multiple identities (and remember the average number in MPD sufferers is eight) even the professionals would be relieved.

What evidence is there to support the genetic theory?

- There are people with Multiple Personality Disorder who have *never* suffered childhood abuse or severe traumas. What caused their extra identities to develop?
- No one can deny that genetic transfer has been a reality for millions of years. Information, skills, and compulsive behaviour— it exists even in species with very small brain capacity. The transfer of such memories is a reality.
- Selective breeding of animals has proved that different traits of character, temperament, and personality can be genetically transferred to following generations.
- Under deep hypnosis, countless individuals have revealed separate "identities." Some have spoken in foreign languages (which they did not learn in their current life) and

accurately described places that no longer exist. (See
Chapter 27 on Past Life Therapy for more details.) This
belief in "previous lives" or "previous identities" also forms
the basis of the belief in reincarnation (See Chapter 25.)
that has existed for thousands of years.
- There is no evidence to suggest that the human brain is
incapable of inheriting ancestral memories, including
identities/personalities.
- MPD sufferers have been known to have scores of alternative personalities, and it is not unusual for them to have
different genders, sexual orientation, names, histories, and
personality traits. It beggars belief that a single subconscious, under any circumstances, could create such a
spectrum of personalities.
- 50 percent of our "ancestral contributors" are male and 50
percent are female. This multi-faceted assembly of biological contributions must have more impact on who we are
than anyone dares guess.
- it is even conceivable that these hidden identities, apart
from being located in the subconscious, play an active part
in the *functioning* of the subconscious during the day or
night. If we relinquish control of the conscious mind when
we sleep, "who" takes control of the subconscious?

I find it reassuring to have the option that these personalities
(in some form or other) are present in our minds, **because it
would be even more frightening for humanity if the
subconscious did have the capability of creating identities at
will. What other powers might it have?**

The professionals must be fully aware of all these factors, but
discount them as being unscientific, unreliable, and unproven.
They say this about other people's evidence, yet they still adhere

to their own list of **unsubstantiated causes.** Their own current literature admits *"there are no known causes of these mental illnesses."*

Progress is being made in constant research on mental issues, but it centres round understanding and treating physical causes of mental deterioration. Knowledge of the harder, nebulous mental illnesses and their treatment does not seem to be advancing, and public response to illness remains that *"suffering from cancer"* evokes feelings of sympathy, whereas *"suffering from depression"* is more likely to evoke impatience.

Surely we should be up to learning about mental disorders, their early symptoms, and methods of treatment. We should be encouraged to realise how widespread depression is in all age groups. Awareness and understanding lead to empathy.

In the interests of their future patients and the public as a whole, I think the Association of Mental Health Professionals should seriously consider a more pro-active approach to educating the public in their field of expertise. It should be an essential part of a nation's future **Health Education Programme.**

Why would Homo sapiens evolve this way?

The human species has been gifted with an outstanding brain, yet many of its members suffer from a fragility of the mind. Why? I did write much earlier in the book: *Evolution does not begin with a finished product in mind. It only discovers what it has produced when it arrives and survives.*

Man's miracle of genetic inheritance included the **collective** (recognisable human appearance) and the **personal** (features), and perhaps an additional *ancestral inheritance*—something that other species have, but not to the same degree.

Could it be that possessing multiple personalities and abilities is merely a freak of evolution? They could be an extension of the magical inheritance memory packages of other species. Perhaps our *genetic core,* which I believe serves as the principal source of our personal qualities, includes these additional genetic identities. Perhaps they form an ancestral pool of memories waiting to be tapped. These hidden identities might influence our mood swings, our irrational moments, the intensity levels of jealousy and violence, and the hidden "reserves" of bravery or calmness that suddenly appear in a time of crisis. We never know what reserves of character we possess until desperate times call for them.

My imagination rolls on: to steal or not to steal; to lie or not to lie; to risk doing something or not to risk. Decisions and actions have to be taken throughout our lives, and I am wondering how our *alter egos* could help or hinder us during such processes.

But one thing is certain. Their presence becomes a source of mental anguish for some. The triggers that activate them deep in our subconscious could well include violence and abuse. Some of us may be more fragile mentally and our conscious strength can no longer dominate the subconscious.

Many will mock my suggestion that we could be born with additional identities in our subconscious. So be it. Yet it is no more derisive than claiming that numerous different identities could be created in a single subconscious by external forces. In the interest of the patients, both lines of thought are worthy of serious consideration.

Researchers have endeavoured long and hard to find clues in our DNA to explain the origins of mental illness. I would like to include this comment by Margit Bumeister, PhD, in 1995 referring to years of research done by the Human Genome Project:

"Gene defects in more than forty inherited disorders have been identified: Neurofibromatosis, Huntingdon's Disease, and Cystic Fibrosis, to mention just a few. We have even heard of specific gene defects causing more common diseases, such as breast cancer and Alzheimer's, but still no word about genes for bipolar disorder (manic depression) or any other mental illness. Why is it so much harder to find genetic defects responsible for mental illness?"

It would be easy for me to say, "Because they lie in genetic transfer and not genetic defects." But that is only the opinion of an unqualified observer. But it sounds logical and believable.

It offers an optional approach to mental and behavioural matters that I have not seen referred to in writing. If there is merit in it, we could consider abuse as the trigger for releasing the identities, and research new techniques for dealing with the "identities." If these identities are a natural, evolutionary development in our species, they need to be accessed and studied in a different light.

These latent personalities might well be a factor in other less serious mental matters. What other evidence is there to suggest that we may inherit more than we imagined and far more than is generally recognised? I think there is plenty.

❉ ❉ ❉

I apologise to the professionals for daring to write this chapter on mental illnesses. It just happened. I hope it will be taken in the spirit it is offered, namely to present a theory which I feel, although unworthy of being presented by a qualified person, may well be offered by an unqualified one.

As the saying goes, "**Leave no stone unturned.**"

Personal Qualities

Because my four brothers and I were completely different individuals, as if assembled by chance rather than produced by the same parents, throughout my life, I have latched on to any topic that suggested clues leading to new ideas as to how we become who we were.

I now realise that, in the past, I spent too much time trying to understand others. That was a mistake. Endeavouring to understand my own qualities would have been a better and more beneficial starting point. But we don't do that, do we? I cannot recall anyone encouraging me to think about it or even offering me some guidelines on the subject.

"Try to discover the person you are and, when you do, learn to live with yourself."

I read that somewhere many years ago and have always felt it to be both depressing and defeatist.

Anyway, discovering the complete you is an impossible quest because you never stop finding out new things about yourself, but that should not stop you trying.

Imagine having to make an honest and accurate assessment of your qualities as you see them. A list is placed on the table and you are required to complete a box alongside each one with

a number from 1 (not applicable to me) to 10 (definitely me) .
. . and your assessments must be as **honest** as possible!

You look down at the list that appears endless:

Affectionate; ambitious; bad-tempered; brave; calm; considerate; cruel; decisive; dependable; determined, evil; friendly; generous; hardworking; honest; intelligent; jealous; kind; lazy; a liar; likeable; loving; loyal; nervous; optimist; perfectionist; pessimist; punctual; reliable; religious; responsible; self-confident; selfish; shy; sensitive; etc., etc., etc. It goes on and on.

Had that been done to me, I think my first reaction would have been amazement at the sheer number of recognisable personal qualities. How does one actually *acquire* them? I don't recall *thinking* I should be honest, reliable, optimistic, or likeable, and I certainly don't recall making any conscious effort to acquire them.

Personal qualities interact to create the unique temperament and character that is you. They are revealed (*or hidden*) via your personality. As you go through life, you find yourself in new or challenging situations that reveal a little more about yourself. These revelations could be surfacing from the subconscious.

I am sure I drifted into growing up, until I joined the Army (in the days of National Service). Then, I came face to face with reality and the need to pay special attention to quite a few items on that list. Strangely enough, although the Army attached importance to a number of them, like punctuality, I cannot recall it drawing attention to *bravery*. We eventually came to realise that **loyalty** *is thinking of others before yourself*, and **bravery** *is placing the lives of others before your own.*" You only discover whether you possess those qualities when the situation requires them.

Few of us would claim to be as perfect as we would like. We

can all do with an improvement here or a change there. Cosmetic surgery exists for those who consider that they require physical improvements. How do we cope with our non-physical imperfections when we become aware of them? Can we undertake any effective remedial action? After all, we take remedial action as soon as we break a limb or have aches and pains. Why not do the same when we become aware of personal inadequacies?

Before anyone attempts to, they should be more aware of what they are facing. Dealing with one's feelings and attitudes requires preparation. We have to do it because, as the ads are always telling us, "**We are worth it.**"

Our personal qualities stem from the mind because that is where we really exist. The mental fortress that is you has four bastions: temperament, character, personality, and intelligence. All the qualities on "the list" are to be found in one or more of these bastions. To help you differentiate between them, I will explain my breakdown. You may disagree with me and form your own ideas.

Temperament

To me, temperament centres round your disposition as a person. Are you moody, do you have a short fuse, are you sensitive and shy, or are you a nervous type? (Can you see where I am going?) Are you calm or excitable and easily lose control of your temper. These all have a strong emotional content in them.

Character

These qualities are connected with reliability, responsibility, honesty, being hardworking and conscientious, and dependability. These are qualities that might describe the core of a person. When asking for a character reference, one would expect such aspects to be covered.

Personality

This is the means by which you reveal yourself to the world. Whether you dare display yourself honestly is another matter. Manufacturing a personality to conceal failings or evil intent is common. If you were to go around a crowded room chatting to people, and were then asked to identify who were the rapist, the paedophile, the psychopath, the con man, the thief, and the convicted serial killer, you would not find it an easy task.

On the other hand, you would be able to identify the nervous or shy one without difficulty, and the hypochondriacs would give themselves away in the second sentence.

Intelligence

This bastion will hopefully allow you to assess yourself and take appropriate action where deemed necessary.

Having given you some basic guidelines as to which factors influence who you are, you may well ask how you use them.

- You could compile a list of personal qualities and write down your own assessment of yourself (*too subjective*).
- Ask your parents or close friends to do it. (*They would be too kind, not wanting to hurt your feelings.*)
- Perhaps the best way would be to invite as large a group as possible of people who know you and work with you, preferably including some you do not get on with, and ask each of them to write their honest assessment of you as a person, your temperament, character, and personality (without consulting each other). You could even provide them with that cue list to jog their memories.

If they completed the task as objectively as possible, you would have an incredible insight as to your public persona. Believe me, favourable or not, such assessments would be worth paying for, because they could be a wonderful wake up call for evaluating who you are and assessing whether it is possible that remedial action is required, or possible, on your part.

A philosopher (was it *Descartes?*) said something like, "An individual is numerous different people: as seen in their own mind; as seen by family and friends; by colleagues and acquaintances; by enemies, and the true person, known only to God".

Of course, you may never have that opportunity to read their opinions. Perhaps one day someone will have the courage and the opportunity to do it properly.

Having done your best to assess your qualities, and before attempting to improve any, you should give some thought as to how you got them in the first place.

The origins of our personal qualities

Opinions will vary considerably as to how you came to possess your qualities. Some will confidently say you acquired all of them as you were growing up. The influence of people, situations, and experiences combined to mould you. This assessment will be particularly relevant when it comes to light that you have many failings as a human being. If you agree or accept this advice, it makes your intended alteration process much easier. You just change your environment and wait for the improvements.

Another view would be that much of who you are is present when you were born. It would have been contained in your *ancestral core.* Just as your physical features owe a great deal to your ancestral line, so do your mental (personal) qualities.

Triplets can be three distinct individuals from an early age. As the weeks and months pass by, their individual natures become more apparent, yet they will all have experienced the same environmental circumstances from birth.

I believe this *ancestral, genetic core* we inherit at birth contains the foundation of our temperament and character. I am inclined to believe that our personality is also influenced by it.

This is not to say that environmental influences have no impact on you. Where you are born in the country might influence your behaviour to a certain extent. Are regional qualities different because of local environmental influences, or could it be that people in those areas are born with their regional differences built into their genetic core? So many questions and possibilities!

For me, the finite argument that we are *born with* character and temperament is that this process is the norm for the animal kingdom. Animals do not choose their character and temperament, and they certainly do not think about their personality. They just put up with what they are born with and do not consider changing. At least, we can change.

A further consideration is not far from the genetic core theory. If it is proved that we are born with something akin to the "memories" of a number of ancestral identities in our subconscious, they could also be a source of some or all of our personal qualities. It might explain the problem of our *conflicting qualities*. "What are conflicting qualities?" you ask.

Examples might be when a constantly cruel person suddenly displays tenderness to an animal; a normally rational person who behaves extremely irrationally; or an extremely selfish person begins displaying generosity. An explanation could be that, at certain times and in particular situations, our "hidden" identities are influencing our conscious self. It's worth thinking about.

With the numerous inexplicable abilities present in the animal kingdom, such ideas are not without precedent.

Can we do anything about our qualities?

I am sure in some cases we can, if we want to. For example, shy or nervous people always want to change, and have to fight hard to achieve it, but those who lash out when annoyed or are consumed by a jealousy difficult to control need professional help.

There will be some who may be beyond help: the psychopath who can commit violent acts with no feelings of remorse, and the paedophile who knows what he does is wrong, but cannot control himself. Such people have deep-rooted mental issues that challenge the professionals.

The normal person could take steps to improve his or her nature. After all, if we can stop smoking, drinking, and gambling, then working on improving some personal qualities should be a piece of cake.

If you seek assistance from the professional community, the help you receive will obviously be influenced by the attitudes of the professionals. If they are confirmed environmentalists, they may tackle your problems differently from professionals who might propose (deep) hypnosis to search for root causes of your problems.

If the mental health community does open up and help educate the public on mental health issues, the stage may be reached when a patient going for psychological assessment or psychiatric treatment begins the appointment by asking, *"Are you an environmentalist or do you believe in genetic inheritance?"* What a great opening sentence that would be!

Parental Feelings

One quality I have not touched upon is the presence, or lack, of parental feelings, particularly maternal. In our species, the presence of so-called *maternal instinct* can range from those who are devoted to their children, those who will look after the children of others, and those not wanting anything to do with children.

Wherever you are on that scale, you will benefit from learning a little more about maternalism in the animal kingdom. One might have expected maternal feelings to be instinctive in the animal world, but they are not.

Instinctive maternal *behaviour* is present in the way they dispose of their eggs, from the turtle laying them in the sand to salmon and frogs laying and leaving them. When it comes to actual hands-on caring for the progeny, parenting levels range from excellent to non-existent. Even in species that normally contain excellent mothers, there will be many who are less enthusiastic at the rearing process. They become involved in the "producing" part only as a consequence of enjoying the mating process, but because they do not possess the desire or ability to care for the young, they neglect or abandon them.

The one lesson we can learn from other species is that no matter what level of maternal feelings exist in an individual, there is no criticism or guilt involved. It is *natural*, not chosen, behaviour.

In the human context, the same could be written about the grandparents' feelings. Some are utterly devoted to their grandchildren, sometimes making sacrifices in moving to a new house (or country) to be near them, so that they can babysit and participate in the joy of their growing up. Other grandparents are nothing like that (as our daughter will testify). Not that they are neglectful or disinterested in their grandchildren. It is just that people are different.

Our daughter was really disappointed when we told her we were going to live abroad. *"What about seeing your grandchildren growing up?"* (The boys were four and six years old). I nearly suggested she send us home videos, but thought it might not go down too well at the time. They have grown up fine without our regular presence, just as my wife and I managed to grow up without ever-present grandparents.

That is the way we are and have never felt pangs of guilt about it. Our daughter understands that (I hope).

Master of the House Mentality

Before moving on to the next topic, I must add a warning for those males with a *"master of the house"* mentality.

Early in our existence, the male was the hunter, procreator, and head of the family; the female was the food gatherer and home provider.

This later evolved into the male being the provider, procreator, and head of the family, with the female looking after the home.

After World War 1, the female gradually became more involved as a provider, and later an essential equal provider.

The next development was that more females, by choice or circumstance, became the sole provider for the family, until the stage has been reached where a high percentage of them are one parent families.

Females are accustomed to being independent, confident, and proud of their achievements. Many are no longer happy with, or dependant on, a "master of the house" presence, and are seeing males more and more as being merely a useful provider of casual sex for pleasure.

With the arrival of ever-more efficient sperm bank systems, and should the future embrace sperm selection, the historical role of the heterosexual male will be further diminished.

Modern man would be well-advised to pay more attention to his personal attitudes and parental behaviour, or the wheels of evolution will roll over him, and he will find himself existing in a society of Amazonian women who consider him useful only as a slave and for sex.

Gifted People 22

We have all heard of the *prodigy* and the *genius*—those possessing exceptional natural capacity of intellect in art, music, science, and mathematics. They are gifted ones with superior memory or understanding, children with marvellous talents that are a cause for wonder.

How is it they are so blessed? Why should their mental capacity and abilities far exceed those of other people? The answer to that is not dramatically important. Nor do I wish to revel in the achievements of the likes of Leonardo da Vinci, Albert Einstein, or Mozart.

My gratitude to them is that they clearly and unarguably demonstrate the wonderful, mysterious potential of the human brain. One is tempted to think that, if they can be born with outstanding minds, there is no reason why all human minds in time could not evolve accordingly. After all, evolution depends on the different, the unusual, and the special to keep evolving.

The gifts of such people are, of course, mental gifts. I haven't heard anyone pounding the table to the effect that their minds were blank at birth. One has to ask what kind of **gifts** they received. Well, they were certainly not physical or hormonal.

Those people were blessed with special mental talents that, fortunately for the scientific community, were identifiable, visible, and quantifiable—rather like admitting that instinct is prevalent in animals.

Scientific minds become absorbed in fathoming out the workings of the brain to accommodate such genius. I am more the romantic and artistic person who revels in the fact that such minds have existed, and those of similar genius are rushing us forward in this technological era.

Scientists love to study the brain of a genius or a serial killer to ascertain what evidence is present to explain the exceptional qualities of its owner. Do they expect to find an enlarged portion here, or a malformed portion there that led to the owner's fame?

So much attention is being attached to the importance of the wiring-up of the brain and how this mechanism is the means by which the brain functions. The brain is our personal microchip. Some would have us believe that all knowledge and abilities contained on that microchip are obtained after birth. The phenomenon of genius and special abilities is an indicator that the chip receives content **before** birth.

Further beacons of this premise are the claims by others of *special gifts*. Psychics, mystics, visionaries, clairvoyants, mediums, telepaths, and those with ESP (Extra Sensory Perception) or photographic memories, to mention but a few. There are so many personal gifts, all mental abilities, about which we know little and can explain less, which nevertheless have allegedly existed for thousands of years. The professionals readjust their blinkers and find it easier to dismiss and mock them. The *"no scientific proof = no existence"* lobby is strong. It is up to the gifted ones to prove them wrong.

We lesser mortals may not claim to have exotic paranormal

abilities, but we might confess to the odd moment of *intuition* or weird sensations of *déjà vu*.

People claiming to have special mental gifts are frequently described as charlatans. Due to the gullibility of ordinary people, many practitioners have been shown to be frauds, and this has helped to decry them all. But many ordinary people do have faith in them, for one reason or another, my mother among them.

She told me the story (many times, I might add) of a gypsy coming to our house selling pegs and charms. I was a four-year old standing by my mother at the front door. The gypsy looked down at me.

"He's a bright boy. He'll go to university," she said. (This was before World War II when about 5 percent of students went on to university.)

My mother always believed her, despite none of my older brothers and sisters doing it. Even when I said to her later that the gypsy probably said that about every child she met at a doorstep, she remained convinced. (Of course, I might only have gone to university because my mother brainwashed me into believing the gypsy was right.)

I include gypsies in my list of memory categories because I do not believe they are all charlatans. This wider category of "gifted ones" has existed for thousands of years. I refuse to accept that not a single one is genuine.

An interesting fact is that people have been known to develop photographic memories and other mental abilities after receiving severe blows to the head. Others born mentally handicapped may possess wonderful, specialised mental abilities in numbers, drawing complex structures after seeing them once, and so on. The cause of their mental handicap had not affected their "special" mental chambers.

It is not beyond belief to deduce that human brains possess the seeds of genius that just need that something to come to fruition. For the fortunate few, it is there at birth with a fully active brain. For the less fortunate, it surfaces because other parts of the brain are not fully functional. Then, when accidents to the head result in additional mental gifts, it could point to the fact—to put it crudely—the correct segments had been exposed or "knocked into place."

All such examples are telling us that potentially we have abilities we don't even know we have, until they are searched for or are needed.

Someone who loses the gift of sight will develop a wonderful sense of touch, smell, and hearing to compensate. The rest of us never develop them because we are made idle through using our eyes to understand what is happening around us. Surely the same principle can apply to our brains. The society that raises us prevents us from drawing on the potential of our brains and memories. It assumes it knows all we need to learn to become useful citizens. This fact may well, if unintentionally, nullify further development of the potential of the human brain.

One hears of our brains being "wired up" to function effectively and how strokes can damage some of the connections that can result in mental and physical handicaps. I saw a television programme that scanned the active parts of the brain of a "genius" during intense mental activity. An interesting conclusion given was that, when solving certain given mathematical problems, he used different portions of the brain to that used in "normal" brains.

This wiring-up process is evidently paramount in the functioning of the brain and memory. If the brain's *normal wiring process* is interfered with—by accident or by nature—then it could produce the connections necessary to access the chambers of genius. (I know those with scientific minds will cringe at this unscientific description, but it does avoid a much lengthier and technical explanation.)

An additional thought is that "genius" presents itself in art, music, sculpture, mathematics, and science, or the ability to think more deeply and clearly than mere mortals. I wonder which factors dictate the areas of genius? Why was Mozart's music so unusual? Why were da Vinci's gifts so numerous? Could their "other identities" have helped them? (Well, they originated from somewhere!)

What of those wonderful souls who devote their lives and fortunes to helping the sick, the needy and the oppressed? Their genius is their generosity in the complete giving of themselves. This is a quality most mortals do not possess.

My aim in discussing the many facets of memory was to highlight the enormous variety and potential of the human brain—and these are the aspects we are trying to understand. And we are learning more all the time. The scientific community should be embracing the potential obviously present in our brains and not dismiss them out of hand because they appear to lack "essential scientific criteria."

It has only been in recent decades that past-life regression has become more significant in the western world. How many undiscovered chambers await us there? The prospect is tantalising. (See Chapter 26.)

We, who consider ourselves to be average people, could have "gifts" within us that remain untapped. Human brains have proved they contain a propensity for special qualities: to love others more than ourselves, to want to improve the quality of life of others, and to aid others. These are all special gifts. All we need is to want to find the key to them in our minds.

Most of all, we must not let the professionals prevent us from believing these personal mental gifts exist. History has shown that science is only right until it has been proved wrong. It takes time and belief to eventually find the truth. I would therefore claim that my theories are right until the scientists can prove they are wrong.

If you analyse yourself and conclude there is nothing special about you, think again. Your special contribution to the world you live in may not have had the opportunity to reach the surface of your consciousness.

How do we tap into them? If you have not been fortunate enough to have a relative or the right environment to trigger them into use, try different activities.

I have written this book not knowing or worrying whether it will ever be published. In its way, it has been my gift in that it has gifted me the greatest pleasure and personal satisfaction in writing it. It might even have delayed the onslaught of Alzheimer's.

Sexual Orientation 23

Life would be simpler if the population consisted of males and females sexually attracted to each other. It would be so calming, less divisive, and more understandable. But sexual inclinations in humans, like most other things about the species, are complex.

It is still not known for certain (scientifically) what **causes** a person to be heterosexual, homosexual, bisexual, transgender, transvestite, or any of the other sexual orientations. There has been plenty of research, but nothing conclusive.

"The determinants of sexual orientation are by no means fully understood."

Research has been directed at proving specific hormonal or DNA differences exist between the sexualities, believing that *"The sex gene is just waiting to be found."* It proved there are no discernible differences in hormonal levels between the sexualities and no identifiable gene patterns or abnormalities.

What do non-scientific people think about their sexual orientation?

- Some gays believe they were born that way.
- Some gays think they *chose* their sexuality.
- Bisexuals believe they have the true sexual orientation of *choice*.

– Heterosexuals don't really give it much thought.

My parents never mentioned sexual matters (at least, not when I was around), and the subject was not in our school curriculum. It was a boys' school and if you wanted to do biology (for exam purposes), you had to walk around to the nearest girls' school for lessons.

Strange how discussing sex can be such an embarrassing duty. I remember when our daughter went to university, my parting words of wisdom to her were,

"You can come home any time and tell me you are pregnant, but please don't come home to tell me you are taking drugs."

That aptly illustrates the depth of *my* parenting skills at that time.

There must be countless parents today who still cannot bring themselves to provide their children with helpful advice on sexual matters, including some whose offspring have different sexual inclinations. This is because they were embarrassed about it when they were young and received little help. Now that they are parents, they need guidance in doing what their parents never did for them.

The situation has improved considerably for non-heterosexuals. In recent decades, they have advanced from having to behave like members of a secret society (for their own protection from public ostracism and the fear of being blackmailed) to the point where they are able to celebrate their sexuality more openly and even have their own public parades in celebration.

Such "openness" in certain cultures would still be foolhardy, and could result in beatings or execution. Such judgments have long been carried out in the name of morality and faith, and will, no doubt, continue.

We may self-righteously criticise such intolerance and cruelty in other cultures, but heterosexuals everywhere can also be guilty of mentally "condemning" behaviour they don't fully understand. It is convenient for them to accept their orientation as "the norm" and any other as a form of sexual deviation. Many still condemn them in their minds because they do not feel "comfortable" about there being other sexual orientations. They need a better explanation than *"they were born that way."*

Why is sexuality so varied?

Sociologists have long been doing research into what determines sexuality. I don't advise you to read up on it because the outcome, they say, is they do not know. So much scientific research into human behaviour contains conclusions that are conflicting and inconclusive, followed by *"further research needs to be done."* And they have been trying to find the answer for over a hundred years!

I believe the general public should be exposed to material and ideas on human sexual orientation. Why? Because lack of argument and debate on the subject only allows ignorance and condemnation to prevail. If the scientific community is reluctant to provide such material, for whatever reason, then it must fall to members of the non-scientific community to get the ball rolling.

Once again, I am fortunate in that I can leave myself wide open to criticism from by discussing in plain English the factors involved, as I see them.

Is sexuality genetic?

Are we born with our sexuality? Well, one thing is certain. I never chose mine. In fact, I never even thought about it. I just grew up and eventually discovered I was attracted to girls. Had it ever crossed my mind, I would have immediately assumed everyone was born that way.

No one told me I should be a heterosexual. I listened to church sermons from the age of twelve to eighteen and the subject of sexuality never came up.

I was twenty years old before I ever heard the word *homosexual*! (Forgive me. I grew up in a different era.) It had to be explained to me (and I did Latin at school!). I couldn't believe it. And the man being pilloried in the papers at the time (the 1950s) was a peer of the realm.

And then when estimated percentages of homosexuals in the general population were given, I couldn't believe that either. I recall sitting on the upper deck of a bus looking around and working out that "percentage" of the people on board and who they might be. You've got it. I couldn't believe it!

If it is genetic, one would think that identical twins would always grow up having the same sexual orientation. Not necessarily. If the parents were heterosexual, how could homosexuality in the family be genetic?

When I discovered that a similar range of sexual inclinations existed in the animal kingdom, I was inclined, at first, to believe it was a natural part of one's make-up at birth. One's sexual orientation is a *natural phenomenon* for the individual, be it animal or human. After all, I hear no one accusing the animals of *choosing* the wrong sexuality.

But then, people say, "Animals are animals, and people are people. There's a big difference." *Is there*?

Is it a question of choice?

From the condemnation of homosexuality and other sexual inclinations by numerous cultures and institutions, there are obviously many who are of the opinion that individuals choose their sexuality and are capable of changing it back to what "it should be," if they were so inclined.

I wonder whether those people demanding that gays "*give it up*" ever considered whether *they* chose their own sexual orientation, or would they have to admit that it just crept up on them, like it did with me.

I also wonder whether they have thought about the matter seriously or are just mouthing what they are told to mouth.

Can anyone seriously claim that a person knowingly and deliberately casts off the cloak of social, sexual conformity to *select* a sexual orientation that might be mocked, despised, and condemned by ignoramuses?

Who would *choose* a sexuality that would be declared illegal, which could lead to blackmail and, in certain countries, could result in vilification and death? Who would choose a sexuality that might prevent them from telling their parents about it?

If virtuous heterosexuals woke up to discover they lived in a predominantly gay society that demanded they immediately become gay (*or else!*), would they be able to comply? What arguments would they offer to remain as they were, except, "*I was born this way!*" They would even appeal to the State to protect their civil right to be heterosexual?

Young readers may feel that it is no big deal being gay, and cannot understand what all the fuss was about? They are right. Over the last fifty years, homosexuality has become (publicly) more acceptable. But there remains considerable discomfort with it, even in so-called "civilised" societies. Why? Because it is still not understood, and religious teachings have not exactly helped.

Religious teachings also prevent people from accepting the theories of evolution, in spite of the scientific evidence. One would think that, as God created us in His image, all sexual orientations were part of His plan or, at least, a consequence of it.

Possibly their denial is as much emotion as faith. Many heterosexuals find it difficult to accept a man kissing a man, or a woman kissing a woman, and even more difficult to imagine what sexual activity they engage in. Even in this more enlightened era, these can be genuine, heart-felt, natural reactions.

To begin to accept its existence is a major step. To accept it being a *natural* act for them comes later. To be comfortable with it may take even longer.

This is why open discussion on the subject will assist in understanding. Then, people who are against sexual diversity or, at least, not comfortable with it, will have facts on which to form their feelings.

In the past, homosexuals were pariahs. Many a public figure lived in fear of his sexuality being revealed. Hitler did his best to exterminate all homosexuals the Nazis could find.

I repeat the question. Who would consciously abandon heterosexuality to become part of the misunderstood minority?

I agree that there is choice in certain instances. Bisexuals are able to conform sexually in any society. They are willing and able to engage happily in sexual relations with males and females.

My first awareness of bisexualism also came at university (shortly after learning that homosexuality existed). Debating was a love of mine and, as it was topical at the time, I made a comment that my landlady was worried because another student and I were in the bathroom together.

After the debate, a male friend asked me whether I was interested sexually in men. I asked him why he would ask me such a question. He said, "If you are, I would be interested."

I had seen him with loads of girls and couldn't understand why he was asking such a daft question. His answer is imprinted on my mind:

"I love sex with a woman, but I would never refuse a man." You've guessed it. I couldn't believe it!

I can now understand a parent (male or female) having spent a "normal" married life deciding at a later stage to "come out" and live with a partner of the same sex. There must be a number of explanations for such a situation. A gay person could have conformed and married and had children, and then when older, and society was more receptive, decided to come out.

A bisexual could live in a heterosexual marriage and, years later, maybe when the children have left home, meet someone special and decide to form a gay relationship. That would not be too difficult a choice for them.

As I said earlier, bisexuals really do have a choice. The question is, "Why are they different from heterosexuals and homosexuals?"

How do we perceive homosexuality?

Today, children at primary school learn about of the existence of homosexuality. In the near future, no doubt, some will advocate teaching it in nursery school. At first, I was opposed to this approach believing it was too soon, but I have changed my mind. I believe that bullying can occur when children become aware of a young person's different sexuality. But teachers need to teach, not only the "what" of sexual inclinations, but also the "why." Otherwise, the bullying will continue.

The image of homosexuality, especially concerning men, has been centred on the effeminate male stereotype whose voice, appearance, and mannerisms are associated with gay people. They are seen as "mincing" down the road, having a limp handshake, and forever using the word *"Darling."* They are the types who, as soon as they are seen, may cause some people to nudge each other and pronounce "knowingly" that they are gay.

This image has misled people for thousands of years—so much so that, when it was announced that Rock Hudson, a famous leading film star, was gay, the heterosexual world was in shock. *"How could he be gay?"* was a common reaction, because he did not fit the public persona of a homosexual.

In fact, the wider public might never have discovered his true sexuality if he had not been dying from AIDS. (His was also the era when such things remained hidden.)

This stereotyping of gays must have led researchers to assume they were different from heterosexuals, perhaps with lower levels of testosterone, but much research shows their testosterone levels are as normal as for all males.

"It must be a difference in part of the brain that affects sexuality." They are still searching for it. There must be a *sexuality* gene that determines whether we are bisexuals, homo-sexuals, or heterosexuals, not forgetting transgender people and transvestites, or the promiscuous ones. No wonder the research is difficult and inconclusive.

The greater the occurrence of well-known personalities revealing they are gay, the greater the confusion. "He looks so normal" is a common reaction. "She is so attractive, why would she be a lesbian?" Or horror of horrors, *"If she likes having sex with men and women, she is a slut!"* Such pearls of wisdom abound in the public domain.

Decorated members of the Marines have admitted being gay. That does not exactly correspond with a limp handshake image!

International football and rugby players have proudly admitted they are gay. Times they are a-changing.

One has to conclude that gay men can be physically similar

to non-gays. Why not? Their testosterone levels are the same. They do not have to belong to the ballet or the theatre. They are often better human specimens (physically) than non-gays because they work out in gyms to make their bodies physically attractive.

I would love a famous, heavy weight boxer or wrestler to "come out." That would put the cat amongst the pigeons!

Are we any wiser or nearer to forming opinions about homosexuality?

– We know that homosexuals, bisexuals, and lesbians are normal, physical members of their gender in every way.

Research has failed to reveal any significant mental or gene variations, either.

The only clue we seem to have is if *some* males adopt an effeminate form of behaviour.

For me, lesbians are even more difficult to pick out. I understand some like short hair and wearing trousers, but so do lots of women.

Let us examine another aspect of sexuality that raises different issues.

Transgenders

A person of one sex genuinely believing they are living in a body of the wrong sex is called a *transgender.* One cannot imagine the thought processes of looking in the mirror and seeing a male (or female) and believing you should be looking at the other gender.

This belief within transgenders is so powerful and desperate that they take active steps to have their body changed to the gender they believe is correct for them.

This conversion is not a simple process and takes many years of counselling and activities to satisfy psychologists, doctors, and all concerned that the individual is both determined and mentally prepared for the physical procedures needed to change the body. To help their body become more masculine or feminine, as required, they are prescribed appropriate hormonal treatment.

It goes without saying that such people must suffer mental turmoil before they take appropriate steps to correct the sexual imbalance in their lives.

Transgenders, and the situation they find themselves in, lead me into believing that accepting the gender we are born with, without reservation, depends on two things.

For most of us, the matter is resolved at birth when we are declared to be a boy or a girl, and we are happy to grow up as such.

The existence of transgenders suggests we must also be born with a *mental* awareness of which sex we are. Most of us, blissfully unaware of the need for any *mental* approval, are perfectly content with the body we received.

As with all forms of genetic inheritance, there is a variance in the effectiveness of the transfer. A percentage of the population must inherit a *mental* perception of their gender that is not compatible with the physical body they were born with.

For the large majority of the population, the mental image and physical body are in harmony, and the individual's gender is accepted without difficulty or, more likely, without thought.

The dominant force determining compatibility or otherwise would be the mental conception of one's true gender. Once again, this situation arises because of the fifty-fifty gender contribution at conception and certain random variations. These could be evident from minor and harmless mental departures from the norm right through to the transgender stage. What sort of "*symptoms*" of non-alignment could there be?

One common example would be the healthy, heterosexual male who enjoys wearing silk underwear, women's clothes and shoes, and maybe even make up. Such behaviour is fairly harmless. They could be excellent spouses and parents, and their families, when they learn about it, accept the little habit as harmless. Such mild forms of cross-dressing give mental and physical pleasure to members of both sexes.

Most heterosexuals would not dream of dressing up in this fashion. But then, that is not to their credit. I mean, it is not as if they reject the option. It just does not occur to them.

A severer symptom of non-alignment would be the transvestite who derives pleasure from wearing clothes and being taken for a member of the opposite sex

Transsexuals are people who like to identify completely with the opposite sex. For example, the men will even have breast implants.

I don't wish to over elaborate on the approaches to the physical image projected by transvestites and transsexuals other than to make the point that their *mental image* of their sexual inclination is somewhat at odds with their body.

It would not surprise me if transgenders and others also exist in the animal kingdom. Obviously, they cannot tell anyone or do anything about it. but it seems logical that if the mental acceptance of one's given gender is an important factor in humans, the condition must exist in animals. It could well be a reason certain animals have no interest in mating or rearing progeny.

There is anecdotal evidence that some hens do attempt to crow, and have even been known to change plumage and produce a coxcomb. Such stories are either a joke played on the media or a physical manifestation of hens believing they should be cockerels, eventually achieving that goal—definitely a case of "mind over matter."

How does all this help in understanding sexuality?

We know that physical attributes such as strength, ability, and bravery are irrelevant considerations in determining sexuality, and *hormonal* levels are no more revealing. The body performs the biological function of providing the sex drive and sexual urges, but it does not determine the source of sexual arousal.

One's gender does not determine one's sexual orientation, and the *mental perception* of one's gender is purely for accepting or not accepting the body received at birth.

Is there another part of our entity that could be that defining influence?

Initially, I considered the defining element in this conundrum, centered around one of the oldest sayings applied to human relations: ***"Beauty lies in the eye of the beholder."***

We must be born with a visual perception of what is sexually stimulating, be it to the opposite sex, the same sex, or both sexes.

Finding people attractive can begin at an early age, but puberty is the trigger for awareness of sexual attraction.

Is it so ridiculous to say, "I am a **heterosexual** guy who *sees* females as beautiful, desirable, and extremely fanciable? I see certain women in my mind and I fantasise about them. I have photographs of them on my locker, etc."

Or how about, "I am **gay** and I find men attractive. I can bump into somebody for the first time and my reaction may be, *"He's gorgeous."*

And we must not forget the **bisexual**. *"I am equally attracted physically and sexually to men and women. My cup overfloweth!*

Such an explanation may not be scientific, but it seemed perfectly reasonable, logical, and very possible. After all, whichever sexual attraction we have is not far removed from personal preferences, such as attracted to particular coloured hair, being a "leg" person, or a "breast" person.

If our brains are wired up to receive and retain images, knowledge, and memories, what is there to deny that those billions of nerve ends, affected by our lineage, are passed on at conception by our parents who went through the same process. If nerve ends control survival of memories in the brain, and we know memories can be passed on genetically, it follows as highly likely that what determines our sexuality is part of that process. I was convinced that **"visual attraction determined one's sexuality,"** until my son-in-law stated the obvious flaw in this reasoning by saying, *"What about blind people? How is their sexuality determined?"*

Back to square one. Not chemical; not DNA based; and now not visual? There had to be an additional factor.

I then imagined the scenario of a person in bed suddenly awakened in the middle of the night by two people getting into the bed, one on each side. The left hand touches a large breast and the right hand comes into contact with male genitalia. The sexual response to that touching would reveal whether the individual was heterosexual, homosexual, or bisexual.

Whereas a person with sight might use the eyes as the principal sense initially in selection, a blind person would be paying attention to the person's voice, choice of words, sincerity, personality, warmth, sensitivity, and even the sense of smell.

The senses are vital in selecting people of interest, but they do not, in themselves, define a person's sexuality.

This being the case, it would suggest that one's sexuality is indeed inherited, and it is our senses (visual or otherwise) that then influence our choice of a partner.

Those who disagree that each person inherits a mental image of what is sexually stimulating, and this determines their sexuality, will continue to search for other answers.

In a society boasting of anti-racism, religious freedom, freedom of speech, and civil rights galore, surely there should be freedom of sexuality.

✿ ✿ ✿

I know there will be readers who will disagree strongly with some of my views on sexuality. Years ago, someone dear to me disagreed so strongly that, when I refused to change this chapter, he did not speak to me for more than two years. Fortunately, we resumed contact before he died. He was my brother.

How Are We Unique?

We are told that physically we are unique human beings. Our face, eyes, ears, walk, blood, fingerprints, and voice are all positively identifiable as being ours. DNA also reveals a great deal about our ancestral line. All these facts and more have been clearly illustrated in various ways.

We are also told that we are unique mentally, but I cannot recall reading or seeing precisely what is meant by that. It is for the professionals in this field to provide such information and guidance to the public. They have failed to do so, and no doubt they have their own very good reasons. No matter how justified those reasons are, whether they are still trying to prove it or fathom it out, or whether they have nothing worth saying, it does not help those of us who may have decided it is time to learn more about ourselves.

The reason I consider greater understanding of our mental uniqueness to be so important is that more clearly defined origins of behaviour could not only be enlightening for us, but might also assist the professionals in providing treatment that is as effective as possible,

Never having undergone psychiatric treatment, I cannot comment on current procedures. But I am of the opinion that their success rate in treating people with behavioural problems or mental disorders cannot be anything worth shouting about, because I have not yet heard or read about anyone "shouting." Of course, I may be dreadfully mistaken in my impression that treatment seems to be more about coping and containment, rather than cure. If the counter claim is that cures are extremely difficult in matters of the mind, I would agree, but add that the same excuse used to be given about curing ailments of the body.

If the official opinion is that psychology and psychiatry is in a healthy state and meeting the needs of patients, then why is this fact not publicised? It would be most reassuring to the general public. If it is not, then maybe they should undertake a rethink, in the interests of the patient, of course.

Have you ever wondered which ingredients go into making you a unique mixture of humanity? I have, and the big questions for me were:
- *what contributes most to our uniqueness?*
- *in what ways?*
- *can we contribute?*

To answer these questions, I need to draw together some of the points I made in earlier chapters.

What contributes most to our uniqueness?

The environmentalists would claim it is "life." You should give serious consideration as to whether they are right. They are intelligent and qualified people who have thought long and hard about the subject and have concluded that the process of *"who we become"* begins at birth when we come into contact with external influences.

They entered their professions because they wanted to help people. They must believe they are right. Are you happy to agree with them that our minds are essentially *clean slates* in the beginning and it is life's experiences that influence us most?

My position differs because, although the environmentalists are to be respected, I believe they are inhibited by their intelligence that demands they need identifiable and verifiable proof of the validity of any theory or fact concerning the mind and human behaviour. It is a scientific straight jacket restricting their mental flexibility.

Obviously, we react to external factors, particularly traumatic events. If the experience results in extreme behaviour or mental disorder, it is scientifically convenient to designate the traumas as being the sole **cause** of them. Suggestions that traumas can trigger the emergence of disorders, but *genetic* factors are also strongly involved, are likely to be dismissed as "scientifically flawed."

Scientists readily acknowledge the existence of instinct and instinctive behaviour in the animal kingdom, even though they cannot explain them "scientifically." I do not doubt that further research will reveal that lower order species have even greater intelligence and more personal qualities than are currently acknowledged. Still, the professionals are reluctant to accept that any such influences contribute to the uniqueness of the human mind.

Because they have concentrated on the impact of life's experiences in all mental problems, I have described their approach as "blinkered" and failing to take into account other potentially important influences.

The ***real origins*** of human behaviour are there to be found, and it should be the mental professionals revealing them.

Am I maligning them when I say they are too obsessed with the negative environmental effects on human behaviour? Am I misrepresenting them when I feel they have built a fence of science around their theories, diagnoses, and treatments, and are determined to sit on it?

Our minds deserve more believable "origins" than the likes of *"housing, parents, education, opportunity, and experiences."*

Genetic Core

Our *ancestral core* is as essential to our mind as bones are to our body. It all begins at that magical moment of conception with the mixture of chromosomes from both parents, just as they received their concoction of chromosomes from their parents, and so on down the hereditary line.

This constant mixing of male and female chromosomes and gene pools down our direct ancestral line, for as long as it goes back, is what produces our very personal and unique mind, just as it does our unique bodies. And this unique combination assists us in becoming the person we are and how we behave. It must also contribute to any mental "anomalies."

When discussing MPD (Multiple Personality Disorders), I hypothesised that the multiple identities surfacing from the subconscious into the conscious were not **caused** by external traumas. The traumas merely **triggered** the emergence of identities already in the subconscious. If so, they had to be part of a genetic inheritance package. The corollary of this is that we must all be born with additional identities secreted in our subconscious.

Even if your initial reaction to this is one of disbelief, don't reject it completely. Butterflies, birds, insects, and others are more than capable of transferring memories to their progeny. Because we claim we don't need genetic transfer, it does not prove that evolution agreed on that point.

If it is so, then it may even be that these *"identities"* and our *genetic core* are both sources of our personal qualities. There could be a case for arguing they are one and the same thing.

What is unique about us?

If we accept that we inherit ancestral mental qualities, we must consider how such a process works. The hereditary factor means "access to qualities from our forebears," and our direct forebears are 50 percent female and 50 percent male. All those chromosomes, genes, neural circuits, memories, and personal qualities are there to be randomly accessed at the moment of conception.

It is the random element in this process that ensures that we are unique, irrespective of any external influences. Imagine all those sperm fighting to reach the egg, each one an individual, each one containing its own particular ancestral combination of qualities to join with those of the egg, and the one that wins becomes you.

Because the influences are randomly contributed by both genders, we should not be surprised that "anomalies" occur in the resulting product. For example, the sexual norm for the majority is to possess minds that are visually and sexually attracted to the opposite gender, but there will inevitably be variations in the outcome. Such anomalies would be:
- *Gays* who have a visual and sexual attraction to the same gender.
- *Bisexuals* who find both genders sexually arousing.
- *Transgenders* who received the "wrong" mental image of the gender they had.
- *Heterosexuals* who derive pleasure from presenting themselves as the other gender (*transvestites*), or happily married men with families, who discover they derive pleasure from wearing women's dresses or silky undergarments.

These, and others, are merely consequences of the many random influences presenting each of us with our own special package, and all of it is evolutionary natural.

What some might describe as "deviation" is simply behaviour that is as randomly natural as possessing blue eyes or a preference for certain colours.

In a way, these numerous qualities are our inheritance and could be termed personal **instinctive** qualities. I use the term "instinctive" more in the sense of *"inclination to be . . . "* or *"have a potential to be . . . "* such as, a born leader, shy or nervous, introvert or extravert, ambitious, self-centred, etc.

The characteristics need not be immediately evident in your nature. Some will be hidden and accessed only under certain circumstances.

For example, some friends may be excellent family men, good neighbours, and popular in the community. Circumstances change and they are encouraged to commit licensed atrocities against others in their community without fear of retribution. Some will consider the suggestion to be repulsive and refuse to participate. Others will volunteer and then enthusiastically carry out the atrocities.

Those who volunteered had accessed a part of their nature they did not know they possessed. The rest did not have the "potential" to commit such acts against other human beings in their mental package.

One would hope that those qualified in understanding the workings of the mind and human behaviour would assist us in understanding our uniqueness and its significance in our personal development. They are the dedicated professionals. It is their opportunity to enlighten us about such matters.

If they are unwilling to communicate more with the public, it would be like admitting that they do not have any helpful knowledge to pass on. I am sure that is not the case. They have many professional straight jacket restraints preventing them because we know, like doctors, they enter their profession to help people. However, they should pay more attention to their image and adopt a more prominent role in today's society.

Can we contribute?

To be able to contribute to who we are would be satisfying, to say the least. Environmentalists push experiences, and Naturists push heredity, so we should be doing our bit.

If we could assess ourselves more honestly and come to acknowledge our positives and negatives, we would be in a better position to influence our so-called "uniqueness."

Looking back over my life, I am convinced that, had I been fortunate enough to have encountered such open discussion and ideas in my formative years, it would have been of great benefit to me as a person.

It may be that we need encouragement and training to accomplish something worthwhile. If we expect others to change their nature, we should ask no less of ourselves.

That is another reason we are unique in the animal kingdom. We are capable of consciously making changes.

At school, I was given the opportunity to debate and to act in school plays. I enjoyed such activities, and have continued doing them over the years. I have never believed the school *developed* those interests in me. There were seven hundred pupils and only a very small percentage debated or acted. My brother had the same opportunities, but different interests.

Things such as this lead me to believe that my love of arguing and acting "were in my package." Those who recoil at the mere thought of giving a speech in public or of being asked to act in a play will have been blessed with a host of other qualities.

Do our emotions contribute to our uniqueness?

The range of emotions evident in humans has considerably more depth and scope than in other species—so much so, that we frequently refer to them as being *human* emotions, which almost implies that other species have only *animal* emotions.

This perfectly natural superior attitude on our part also encourages us to assume that personal qualities must be lacking when instinct is the driving force in a species, particularly in something as lowly as insects. "They cannot possibly possess emotions!"

We cannot let ourselves believe we are the first to evolve with such emotions as anger, jealousy, greed, fear, sorrow, and love. Even primitive species in the sea experience *anxiety* when danger may be present and *fear* when it is. They can be *excited* at the prospect of obtaining something desirable and *annoyed* when personal territory is invaded. "What will be emotional responses for us must be instinctive reactions for them." Once again, I find myself claiming that if insects can inherit knowledge, skills, and memories, then emotions could well be inheritable.

If they have emotions, then they inherited them. We can therefore conclude that genetic transfer in the animal kingdom, not only involves instinctive attitudes, it also includes emotional feelings.

We have abundant experience of emotional behaviour in domesticated animals. One only has to observe them to witness displays of love, selfishness, generosity, caring, self-sacrifice, guilt, loyalty, empathy, joy, and grief. We may disagree on certain specific emotions present in animals, but I am sure we would all agree that non-human animals possess an abundance of them. So, they are not just **human** emotions, and we are not the first to possess them.

From primitive species to more advanced ones, animals are born with a built-in emotional package. It stands to reason.

It follows that humans also receive a specific concoction of emotional content in their mental package, and as with other elements in that transfer, there would be a random factor. To ignore this possibility is like denying the theory of evolution. An important, additional variable would be the *level* of emotional intensity (or lack of it) that an individual inherits. This helps to explain why some lucky ones are capable of being loving, caring, and compassionate, while others are emotional deserts.

Another example would be feelings of *jealousy*. Human males faced with a similar jealousy-provoking situation can react in a variety of ways. One might sit down saddened and bewildered, another might storm out of the house in a temper, while a third could go berserk with jealousy and commit an act of violence.

Perhaps more surprising is the origin of our likes and dislikes. Although these can be influenced by our experiences, they also contain what could be termed "anomalies."

Personal likes and dislikes

This can be an interesting topic to think about. We can all understand it when someone is exposed to classical music or modern jazz and comes to love it, or someone has an unfortunate experience in water when young and does not want to swim. These are all perfectly explainable.

I am talking about personal reactions to things or situations without ever having had any experience.

For example, one of my brothers disliked all sports at school and never participated in any of them. I grew up loving all sports. There was only a sixteen-month age gap between us, and we were of similar build.

I had one dislike that stayed with me for sixty years. I could not drink alcohol. As a student, I worked in a pub in the evenings and people would buy me drinks. Friends said beer was an acquired taste, so I kept trying, but I even ended up unable to drink a shandy, because I could still taste the beer. Similarly, with spirits. I have never acquired a taste for whisky, gin, or brandy. Everyone in my family enjoyed drinking, and most of my student friends "loved a pint." Yet I went through student years and twenty-three years in the Army drinking soft drinks. I would not say I was a social outcast because of it, but you can imagine the reaction of some of my new "peers" when my response to their offer of a drink was to ask for an orange juice or coca cola.

I did not come from a religious family, and none of them had any alcoholic tendencies (that I knew of). I was about sixty years old when I began drinking wine with the evening meal.

Believe me, if I could have liked beer or spirits, I would have drunk them. And I am not alone in having inexplicable dislikes. My only explanation (to myself) was that it was not in my mental package from the beginning. Perhaps an ancestor was anti-alcohol. So, why did *he* have to be in my package!

You may well still disagree with me that so many personal qualities, such as character, emotion, and even ancestral memories, can be part of the outcome of the male sperm joining with the female egg, but it does in the animal kingdom and we are part of that.

I must add that we are mentally far more capable, complex, and unique, but this only convinces me that all that I have been expounding about genetic transfer is only the tip of the iceberg.

Gathering the Threads of Ancestral Memory

By now, you will have become convinced that I have gone overboard about genetic transfer in the animal kingdom. In various chapters, I have discussed the significance of instincts, our genetic core, past lives, inherited personal qualities, ancestral memories, and additional inherited identities in various contexts.

If I am lampooned professionally for my ideas, it will still be up to you to make up your own minds. Your major decision will not be whether I am right or wrong, but whether you find you are *interested* in the origins of human behaviour and want further informed information.

I would like to draw together the *threads of my ideas* to explain the journey that convinced me there were sufficient grounds to believe that, not only did logic appear to be on my side, but also that my unscientific opinions were worthy of being put down in writing.

There will be many qualified people who will refute any suggestion that ancestral memories and identities can be genetically transferred, along the lines suggested in this book. That is understandable, and to be expected, but the chances are they will be the same people who are unable to explain how *instincts* work or who insist there is nothing worthy of consideration about material emanating from past life regression and, even more likely, are still convinced that additional identities in sufferers of Multiple Personality Disorder are created by severe trauma. If that is the case, then I believe you should feel fairly relaxed about making up your own mind.

I cannot claim I am right about ancestral memory and its impact on human behaviour, but I can describe certain milestones on my journey that may help you in the process of forming your own opinions.

The beginning

The beginning for me was when I realised that **instincts** were *inherited memories that influence animal behaviour.*

The use of the word *"memories"* is deliberate because that is precisely what is being genetically transmitted: the transfer of specific information and emotions from one mind to another.

The numerous examples in the animal kingdom of miraculous instinctive behaviour, where even the most insignificant insects possess amazing ancestral gifts, would make anyone marvel.

We know that *species memories* (which we have come to call instincts) are successfully passed on from one generation to the next. We can surmise that the "mechanics" of this achievement is by genetic transmission (*neurons* and *neural networks*) processing relevant information.

The natural progression from there was to conclude that *personal* qualities were also handed down to progeny, both physical and mental. Animals do not *choose* to be dominant or docile, just as they do not choose their sexual orientation. Their motto might almost be, *"What I have is what you see, none is manufactured 'cos it's all just me."*

This naturalness, in some cases, even extended to not being maternal (European cuckoos), or not being afraid of humans (robins). Emotional responses and personal levels of maternal feelings all appear to be in the mental package. We also know that temperament, character, and intelligence are vital considerations in animal breeding programmes.

What about humans?

Seeing such essential features in all other species as being entirely natural, it came as a bit of a surprise to be told that we are completely different. *"We are not like the rest of the animal kingdom. We are moulded by society; and who we are is a reflection of the environment we were brought up in and the experiences we have had to face, and that is how it will be until it can be proved and validated to the high scientific standards we require, that there are other, better explanations."*

Actually, those words are mine, but that is my perception of the prevailing professional view, but I could be entirely wrong about that, of course.

What led me towards *human* "ancestral" influences?

Having been impressed by some of the origins of behaviour in the animal world, naturally I felt that humans must be influenced, to some extent, in a similar fashion. I couldn't imagine evolutionary processes suddenly being discarded when we came on the scene, so I must have been looking for clues to indicate we were genuine members of the evolutionary tree.

I read about **past life regression** several decades ago, and I concluded that the considerable documented results of deep hypnosis sessions were worthy of some respect. If reports are to be believed, poorly educated farmers speaking in archaic French or descriptions of locations which had to be verified by local historians because they no longer existed, struck me as being worthy of more consideration than being dismissed as "influenced by the therapist's questions and the product of the patient's reading or watching television."

It no longer surprises me that professionals find it easy to dismiss the theories of others, yet find their own questionable theories easy to justify.

However, I would agree with them that patients undergoing past life regression are not describing events from *their own* "previous lives." I find recounting details of one's own "previous existences" to be less believable, even though I could see why reincarnationists would want it to be that way.

The more believable explanation to that conundrum for me is that patients under deep hypnosis provide information about the lives of some of their forebears. Genetic transfer of memories in the animal kingdom convinced me that the evolutionary "mechanics" existed and, with the potential of the human brain, I considered the transfer of human memories as being more than a possibility. How they are received and dealt with in the subconscious is a matter for the scientists to determine. But if the professionals can claim that the subconscious **creates** identities as a result of severe traumas, I can declare that the subconscious **receives** and **stores** identities genetically.

Influence of mental disorders

I had long thought that, because my wife's phobia of cats did not appear to be of her making, it could best be explained by some hereditary factor. I was becoming more and more receptive to the idea that we could be inheriting more than we might expect.

When reading about **Multiple Personality Disorder (MPD)** I found I just could not accept the logic in statements explaining the causes of MPD, such as:

  - *"Traumatic memories and feelings that go into the subconscious and then emerge in the form of separate identities."*
  - *Repetition of stressful situations at different times help to create different identities."*

Such explanations seemed to be openly declaring that there was no clear understanding of the causes of MPD, but this was the best *straw* they could cling to.

It made me cringe to think that scientific minds, so insistent on "proving and validating," could accept the theory that you can throw memories of traumatic experiences into a pot and out pop a multitude of highly individual, additional personalities.

The consequence of this reaction was, if **external** factors impacting on the subconscious were unlikely to **create** a selection of new identities and personalities, then the source of them must inevitably be **internal**. And what could *possibly be* the origin of a selection of identities, male and female, of individual personalities, and sexual orientations *conveniently* located in the subconscious?

To me, the prime suspect was *ancestral memories*. It ticked all the boxes:

  - Genetic transfer of memories would be into the subconscious.
  - It explains the varied selection of identities encountered in MPD.
  - It also explains why there are sufferers of MPD who have **not** had traumatic experiences.

– A pool of ancestral memories/identities/personalities could be accessed for "contributions" towards our individuality and uniqueness?

- Ancestral memory is a more believable *straw* than those currently offered by the professionals.

I do not believe that this explanation of the natural existence of additional identities in the subconscious is a piece of original thinking on my part. It must have been suggested to, and rejected by, the professionals before now. Perhaps it is rejected because it cannot be "proved and validated."

But surely it has been as proved and validated as *instincts* in the animal kingdom. Instincts have not been "explained" by the scientific community, but are acknowledged because they are known to exist, their influence on behaviour is evident, and their origin is known to be genetic transfer.

Additional identities are also known to exist and their influence on behaviour is self-evident. They are very real and very human personalities. The point in question is whether they too have genetic transfer as their origin, or whether they are individually **created** by separate traumas impacting on the subconscious. Many "professionals" will advocate the latter, which is why I feel their intelligence and training may have dulled their intuitive senses. To deny the potential of the human brain to inherit any significant ancestral features is as illogical as it would be to deny the ability of the rest of the animal kingdom to inherit instincts. Furthermore, to proclaim that external factors are the principal contributor to who we are and how we behave is as illogical as insisting that the environment determines the character and behaviour of all species.

Ramifications of possessing ancestral memories

Assuming that ancestral memories are the source of additional identities in Multiple Personality Disorder sufferers, it stands to reason that possessing such hidden "identities" must be a *natural* phenomenon for our species. Part of our *ancestral core*, our genetic package, includes numerous personal influences, one of which would be ancestral memories

If this is so, it would be of a random nature. Some of us would have more "influences" than others.

If our personal package did contain a number of ancestral identities, they would not be there simply to emerge into the conscious state of unfortunate MPD sufferers or those with other mental illnesses. They would have to be of greater significance than that.

It always amazed me that we are able to acquire so many "personal qualities" without trying or even being aware that they were developing. As I said earlier, it is almost as though *"we evolve in our own little bubble."* So, it was natural that a further logical deduction for me was that the existence of such identities in the subconscious could also be influential in the development of our temperament, character, and personality as we grow up. Subliminal access to our *diverse* range of ancestral memories would explain how members of the same family could grow up with such different temperaments, characters, and personalities.

Can we identify possible influences?

Without doubt, the most significant "influence" would be that which determines our sexual inclination. I am confident that what our eye finds sexually stimulating determines our sexual orientation. Visual attraction is a personal, mental item. If it cannot be proved that chemical or DNA factors are the cause, then *inheriting the memory of what is attractive* is a worthy alternative.

Another indication, for me, would be the mystery of how five brothers could be so different in every sense of the word, or how young people display a keen interest, from an early age, in specific activities such as sport, music, and dancing, while others display no interest in any of them. Such reactions occur naturally without "environmental" influences.

Agoraphobia and claustrophobia are distressing disorders involving the fear of suffering panic attacks. Although there are numerous theories, the experts are not sure what causes them. However, panic disorders are known to run in families. These and other phobias may well have genetic origins.

There are numerous mental conditions that are prefaced by *"the exact causes are not known."* I believe that genetic causes should be much higher on the research agenda.

True or false?

Many will say the whole idea of ancestral memories is all a load of unscientific conjecture, and they would be right. However, it is not being presented as something comparable to Isaac Newton's Laws of Gravity, is it?

This book is written by an unqualified writer for unqualified readers in the hope that it will develop their interest in human behaviour, but most of all to encourage them to *think* more about what makes us tick. If I am a madman spouting mad ideas, does it make you want to know answers that are not "mad"?

If it does, you would then expect the professionals in the mental health community to provide expert information about the current state of mental health, and await their intended proactive actions resulting in greater public awareness of, and empathy for, mental health care.

The medical profession has a highly respected position in our society.

What do we think of the mental health profession? Do we even think of them, never mind respect them? Now is your chance to make a difference.

PART THREE – ADDITIONAL ISSUES

This section looks at subjects that, although not generally portrayed as *part* of us, can certainly be considered influential in the lives of millions.

Reincarnation 26

Religious faith has been a major influence in most cultures and social systems. Its power has always influenced human thinking and behaviour. Those who truly believe have an additional inner strength. Those who do not believe have to rely purely on their own personal qualities and strength of mind to cope with all that life throws at them. Christianity and Islam are two prominent religions with many similarities.

Another influence, present in a number of religions and cultures, which focuses on the existence of a personal soul or life force, is the belief in **Reincarnation.**

Reincarnation is the acceptance that, on the death of the body, the soul transmigrates to, or is born again in, another body.

This belief, in one form or another, has existed in primitive societies and numerous ancient religions up to the present day. Billions of people, some belonging to faiths opposed to the concept of reincarnation, embrace it.

No matter which era one examines, there has been acceptance of the existence of "the spirits." Even in the earliest social groups, they understood that a dead body was lacking an essential ingredient of *life*. They did not know what it was, but they knew it was powerful. It had the power of life over death.

They feared it, prayed to it, and even made sacrifices to appease it. Above all, they respected it. Only later would it be referred to as the *soul*, the *essence*, the *spirit*, or the *life force*.

The whole concept of survival after death, in any form, has great appeal. It rejects the possibility that we exist only once. It refutes any suggestion that, after this life ends, all that we are is extinguished for eternity.

Belief in reincarnation, like the Christian belief in the soul ascending to heaven, offers hope and it promises that there is a purpose and meaning to life. Most of all, it promises that death is not the end, just another beginning.

Without such promises, without such heart-lifting expectations, the dying words of the countless, suffering billions over the millennia would certainly have been: ***"What has been the point of it all?"***

The world is a better place with religious faiths than without them. I believe that because of the humanitarian work performed by believers worldwide, because of the comfort they offer the multitudes needing comfort. I believe it because, without the succour of religious faith, billions would not have been able to cope mentally with the burdens faced in their everyday lives.

Billions of downtrodden masses around the world would have been far more resentful and rebellious about the fact that so many others had so much while they had so little.

Today in India, the caste system is as strong as ever, particularly in large rural areas. The cement keeping the castes contentedly in their correct place is the belief in reincarnation. *"By accepting your correct place in society, no matter how difficult or unpleasant it may be, you will be reborn into a better life."*

I wish to discuss reincarnation as a concept, not as a belief. Then, I will go on to explain which factors may have given it some credibility.

Reincarnation as a concept

The idea of a *soul*, a *spirit*, an *essence,* or a *life force* leaving the body at the time of death is one thing. (After all, it is a cornerstone of the Christian and Moslem faiths.) That it then moves (*transmigrates*) from one body to another is a giant leap for me to make, not because it clashes with the teachings of the faith in which I was raised, but because it immediately raises practical questions for me.

Are we to believe that the body *receiving* a "transmigrating soul" does not already possess a soul or spirit or life force of its own before or after birth? I find this difficult to accept.

When the number of new births exceeds the number of recent deaths, what problems arise in finding a recipient body? This is a practical question because the earth's annual birth rate has been and will continue to be greater than the death rate for a long time. Without wishing to appear facetious, it is not rocket science to calculate that the number of available life forces can never keep up with the "needs" of an ever-increasing world population.

Some beliefs resolve this problem by introducing non-human members of the animal kingdom into the reincarnation cycle. For example, someone who has led a wonderful life will be re-born with more advantages in the next life, whereas a bad person will be reborn lower down the scale, perhaps as an insect.

I have difficulty visualizing the process by which an ethereal life force, not only has to overcome the logistical problems involved in locating a new host, but also has to *decide* whether the next host is up or down the scale. Does it have to search or is it drawn towards a body? Can a human life force be absorbed into a non-human, and vice versa?

When did the process of reincarnation begin? Was it there at "the beginning" or did it evolve as a life force process?

There are so many practical problems preventing me from accepting reincarnation, yet countless intelligent, religious people believe in it. Is it their intelligence guiding them to it, or is it merely a natural hope that life must have a purpose and a future.

Unfortunately, I have not had the opportunity of asking such questions to a believer in reincarnation. I am sure they would have answers perfectly acceptable to them. Hundreds of millions still fervently believe it. It is the linchpin of their lives and far greater minds than mine have considered the relevance of reincarnation and have come to accept it.

As I said earlier, I do not wish to give the impression that I am attacking the concept of reincarnation. To be honest, I feel it has more going for it than some of the Christian teachings that for centuries has used the *carrot* of eternal life in Heaven and the *stick* of the fiery depths of Hell.

Christianity also includes the sacrifice of Jesus as proof that life after death is a reality.

What evidence is there to encourage our acceptance of reincarnation as a reality in our lives?

How did the concept of reincarnation begin?

You will not be surprised to hear that nobody knows how it all began. Because no deity or visionary is on record as having specified that it is a reality, we do not have a starting point for reincarnation. It has simply evolved over the millennia. *"Rein-carnation offers justification for the unfairness of life. This unfairness we now suffer is merely part of a journey. It is but a segment of the cycle of rebirth. Our lives and our destiny are not meaningless. What may be anguish in this life could be rewarded with joy in the next."*

That explanation reads to me like the words of a politician asking people to support him in this election and he will make my life much better after he has been elected. But isn't that the case for all faiths?

One cynical possibility is that it originated at a time in history when the majority of people were poor, downtrodden, and oppressed. (When was that never the case?)

The rich, intelligent leaders of such millions "facing the unfairness of life" conceived a scheme to calm the masses. They did not offer them money and improved lives. They went one better and offered them eternity.

"This horrible life you are suffering is merely a part of your long journey in life. Your current anguish could be rewarded in the next life. But you must **prove yourselves worthy** of achieving a better life by accepting the hardships of this life. Your current misery is because you behaved badly in your last life."

The idea was accepted because their leaders vowed it was true. What else did the poor have to hope for? The concept of death is frightening, but the possibility of absolute obliteration in a single breath is even harder to contemplate after a life of poverty and despair.

Today in India, the cement keeping the castes contentedly in their correct place is the belief in reincarnation.

I feel uncomfortable because I am projecting myself as a cynic. What makes me right when millions of others think differently?

Reincarnation highlights a powerful, inner need we have to believe in something spiritual. Early Man worshipped the sun and the moon, the power of the gods in controlling lightening and volcanoes, and a special power that looked after us. They were all inexplicable phenomena and their mysteries called for acceptance in this world.

Confucianism achieved a similar result in China for centuries. He clearly laid down how each person should behave in relation to family, their position in society, and respect for the State and its officials. The individual's personal goal was to achieve the highest standards of personal behaviour and thus be worthy of the respect of others. According to the Confucian code, all occupations from the poorest peasant farmer to the highest government official, if lived with acceptance, application, and honour, were as praiseworthy as being the emperor. Confucius did not offer an afterlife, but he did add significance and dignity to the life of even the lowest peasant.

Reincarnation, Confucianism, and other beliefs like them, irrespective of their origins, served as valuable tools to preserve social order and the existing social hierarchy. If that had been the original intention, it could not have been more effective.

These systems and concepts became the fabric of societies and an essential aid to orderly government. You were born into your place in life and accepted it. In other words, "rocking the boat" of orderly society would only prove your unworthiness in the eyes of others.

The communists updated this concept. They determined what constituted the correct social order and those who did not accept it or who were classed as unacceptable elements (revolutionaries) were sent immediately to corrective labour camps. Instead of the carrot being *"hope for a future life,"* social order had substituted *"love of the State (and fear for this present life)"* as being the bastion of their social order.

As time has proved, authoritarian methods have a much

shorter control span of the masses than the promise of an afterlife.

Many scientists and evolutionists do not believe in an afterlife. They consider religious faith as a placebo for the masses. *"God did not create Man; Man created God."*

However, many scientists and evolutionists do believe in the existence of a deity, albeit not necessarily as explained in existing religious texts like the Bible. Despite the magnetic attraction of evolutionism, they still find themselves drawn to the belief that so much wonder and beauty in our world might not have been *entirely* due to the irresistible forces of nature and evolution.

This proves that, with all the existing evidence before us, brilliant scientific minds cannot even agree on this point.

The question still has to be answered. "Was the belief in reincarnation merely a cynical ploy to get the peasant masses to accept their miserable lives and not rise up against authority, or was there evidence to support the theory of reincarnation?

It must be strange to be somewhere in a cycle of life, not knowing your previous lives, but striving for perfection in this one to be worthy of a better one next time, and never knowing whether you achieved it.

Religious beliefs have a defined history behind them, whereas reincarnation does not.

There had to be significant reasons leading to the emergence and continuation of adherence to the concept of reincarnation. They were given proof that "previous and future lives" was a reality.

Past life Regression

If you are a Christian, you believe in an *afterlife* as laid down in the Bible, and the resurrection of Jesus is the proof of this.

Transmigration of the soul (*reincarnation*) not only promises life after death, but it also claims you had lives **before** your present one.

Such a claim could not have survived millennia without some credible evidence to place before the billions of believers. While it has obviously satisfied them, the advocates of reincarnation have been unable to supply sufficient evidence to persuade the western scientific community to consider it seriously.

I mentioned *Past Life Regression* (PLR) earlier in the book. I refer back to it now because I believe it has a bearing on the possible origins of reincarnation and its continued existence.

PLR is considered by many to be undeniable proof that reincarnation does take place, so we should examine it in more detail to determine whether it could have a valid connection.

Past life experiences are revealed in western societies mainly under deep hypnosis. The patient is asked to regress gradually to the earliest point in their lives they can remember, and then go back further to a "previous" life. If they do recall one, the hypnotist asks questions that can result in them revealing details about people, places, and events in the past. The whole session is normally recorded.

Amazing details of some "lives" have been revealed by means of past life therapy. Thousands of people have undergone this process. Some have talked in foreign tongues (e.g., old dialect of French) or described places and events in the past that, because they no longer existed, had to be verified by experts or local historians. Nor was regression restricted to only one life.

These so-called results, and many more like them, are not accepted by the scientific community on a number of grounds including:
  – hypnosis is not a reliable scientific tool
  – hypnotists could well be suggesting things to the patient during the session
  – the patient's past life *experiences* could well be a concoction of things they have heard, read, or even seen on television during his or her lifetime.

The scientists do not accept such findings because it is not possible to conduct deep hypnosis under scientifically acceptable "clinical conditions." I would accept that as a fair comment, but does it still justify rejecting **all** recorded results of **every** session? If the report of the farmer speaking an old dialect of French is true, how could he have acquired that from books or television? Surely he would have been of interest to the scientists before they put on their straight jackets.

Despite the failure to impress and persuade modern-day scientists that past life regression is a significant revelation about the potential workings of our minds, advocates hold on to the belief that, if a hundred people attempt to jump a bar eight feet high and only one achieves it, attention should be paid to the single achiever and not to the ninety nine failures, because that is how we learn more about our potential.

Origins of belief in reincarnation

It is more than possible that religious leaders and medicine men of ancient times had their own means of discovering so-called "past lives." Hypnotic or drug-induced trances would have been within their capability. If they heard revealing details of what came to be thought of as "previous lives," they would not have mocked them out of hand. They would have been impressed and accepted them as proof of a previous life. Such events may well have started the reincarnation theory or confirmed its existence.

If the **scientists** dismiss **all** information about previous "lives" recorded on tape by the hypnotists, is that not unscientific, even though they may have some valid objections for not accepting the PLR claims in total? Hypnosis is not a reliable scientific medium, and those under hypnosis can be led into giving specific responses. But scientists should not dismiss all the findings obtained under deep hypnosis, particularly when some of them have been obtained by highly qualified professionals in their own profession. Hypnosis may not be the perfect scientific tool, but it is still a tool worthy of some respect, and one frequently used by psychotherapists in treating patients.

Some of the details and information obtained during "past life therapy" are dramatic and amazing and should not be rejected out of hand.

Mind you, "scientists" have always been keen disbelievers of anything unproven and not validated. Until the laws of gravity were known, proven, and understood, they insisted that the earth was flat. Oops!

So, if one side claims there is clear evidence of a person's past lives, and the other says it is scientifically unreliable, does Past Life Regression reveal anything about our minds or ourselves that might be more believable?

Possible Significance of Past Life Regression

I liken the scientists' attitudes over PLR to their explanations of the existence of multiple personalities. They just don't know. They do not have scientific answers, so they deny its existence. That does not necessarily mean they are right.

Declaring something to be connected with *previous* lives may be immediately rejected without hearing any evidence because many people do not believe in past lives, and the scientific community already rejects the concept of reincarnation.

My conclusions

As I said in an earlier chapter, I think there is another explanation of "past life" regression, and it begins with its description. I do not agree with the hypnotists if they are claiming that patients under deep hypnosis are revealing details of *their own* "previous lives."

I am inclined to believe that what patients reveal when under deep hypnosis is not information relating to their past lives, but memories they have inherited of the lives of their forebears. If this is the case, it should be called **Ancestral Memory Regression.**

The debate would then be mainly concerned with the *possibility of inheriting ancestral memories* and not the impossibility of revealing details from one's "previous lives."

Accessing "memories" under deep hypnosis is an accepted procedure, and an increasing number of therapists are using it in the treatment of patients, particularly over phobias.

In Chapter 20 on mental illnesses, I suggested that multiple identities in a person were not **created** by physical and sexual abuse or other severe traumas, but were ever-present in the mind of the patient, and that it was most likely that we all have other "identities" in our subconscious. The likely cause of this was that they came from our bloodline and were inherited *memories* of previous identities of our forebears.

If this is the case, then the same explanation could well apply to the memories of *"previous lives"* being revealed under past life regression hypnosis. These so-called memories would not be personal (i.e., experienced by the individual), but would be recalling memories of one's forebears.

If this were to be true, as with all inherited aspects, they would be a random selection "from the past." Some recorded PLR sessions dealt with details from centuries ago.

Such an explanation is no more amazing than claiming that a Monarch butterfly inherits complete details of a five-month migration of which it and all Monarch butterflies would only complete a small segment. (I keep referring to that, don't I?)

The brain's neural circuitry capacity, with its billions and trillions of combinations and pathways, is quite capable of secreting images of the lives of past members of our lineage. If the brain can protect the most ancient memories of my hundred-year grandmother when all other memories had faded, it can better protect a butterfly's brain and secrete memories and personalities from our ancestral chain.

The instinctive memories that have been the backbone of species for millions of years have been passed down to countless future generations. The evolutionary process has played its part in this, and it could be but a short step from animals inheriting memories of what to do, to humans inheriting memories of what has been done in the past. **After all, is that not a defini-**

tion of "instinct"?

Our brain has an incredible ability to deal with and recall our own memories. Who can categorically say that it does not have the capacity and capability for dealing with inherited memories from those in our families who went before? Not the scientists, because they refuse to accept the possibility and are not investigating it!

Where Is Evolution Leading Us?

The animal kingdom includes thousands of species that have existed for up to two hundred million years. They are still here because they have been able to live in harmony with their environment.

Our species has existed less than two hundred thousand years. For most of that time, it also lived in harmony with Nature because its limited numbers allowed it. But now it is progressing and evolving too rapidly for Nature to keep up with its demands. We should be asking the question, *"Where is it all leading us?"*

First, I should clarify what I mean when I say *Homo sapiens* is still evolving. A few obvious signs are:

Physically, we are still developing. We are growing in stature, healthier, and living longer.

Our **capabilities** are definitely improving. Fifty years ago, there was great excitement worldwide when a man ran the mile for the first time under four minutes. It is now down to three minutes forty-five seconds. Corresponding improvements have been made in all athletic activities.

Inventive capabilities have brought us into a world that could not have been dreamed of a hundred years ago. The species has come a long way since those days when it believed the world was flat.

Medicine has produced countless benefits for humans. The eradication of major diseases, the reduction of child mortality rates, the doubling of life expectancy, and the future benefits of stem cell research are just a few advances that present the world with incredible population challenges in the coming centuries. From the world being a large place, we can now witness in a second, events occurring twelve thousand miles away, or be in constant touch with whomever we please whenever we wish. The brain appears able to absorb new knowledge and inventiveness, but is revealing signs of an increasing inability to cope with the increased stresses of life.

The numbers experiencing depressions and associated illnesses in the western world are forever on the increase. This is one area where our amazing progress is exacting a cost.

We are told we only use 10 percent of our brain. What exists in the other 90 percent, because we must assume it is not there without purpose? Perhaps that remains for later generations to resolve, if they have the time and inclination.

Many of the questions the medical profession was asking not so long ago have been answered. Now the mental health profession will be expected to get its house in order before finding out what that remaining 90 percent brain capacity is all about. *"Will we give ourselves the time to do these things?*

One aspect of our evolutionary progress has been an increasing capacity for destruction. Our adversarial nature has not diminished, and our means of mass destruction have increased. Instead of adopting the nature of those long-surviving social insects, we have turned into voracious dinosaurs, and we all know what happened to them.

Killing animals used to be Man's means of survival, and then it became his sport. Finally, killing has evolved into gratuitous murder of fellow humans. Even the lowest of animals do not do that.

We are even trying hard to destroy the planet. We desecrate the land, depopulate the sea, and contaminate the air.

The world population has reached seven billion and still increasing with wild abandon. It will soon be ten billion, rapidly advancing to fifteen billion.

Our evolutionary wheel rolls along and, unfortunately, we have the capability of speeding it up. Add to this our inclination to mistrust and hate, and our propensity to destroy and eliminate, and we should begin fearing that our evolutionary progress could be driving us to man-made extinction.

None of this is new. Everyone knows we are failing as individuals, which has led to failings as nations. Setting up of the United Nations after World War 2 produced a spark of hope for humanity, but it has never turned into a flame

What will save us or, more likely, who will save us? Not the politicians or the military, because it is they and their ilk who have created the current pessimism. And I cannot see the nations of the world uniting to demand world peace, even in a crisis.

I have come to the conclusion that our future may well rest with the **mental health profession.** They have to assume the mantle of returning sanity into the world. They have to accept that they and their professional colleagues around the world are the ones qualified to deal with the madness that has brought us to the *status quo.* Pinning hopes on finding other inhabitable planets is no answer.

Homo sapiens has got to take a good look at its present state. But first, we need to have a common belief in the origins of the individual's behaviour because therein lies the origin of the species. If the professionals cannot accomplish that, they will have **little** chance of advancing the mental strength of the species, and no chance of persuading the world to return to the principles that helped other social species to survive for millions of years *"living in harmony and unity with their environment."*

If the psychologists, psychiatrists, and researchers can achieve this, this will definitely become known as their century,

Summary of Major Opinions and Conclusions

At the end of a book like this, it may be useful to provide a summary of main opinions and conclusions. It will help the reader to recall important issues on which they found themselves agreeing or disagreeing with me.

Why was this book written?

I began writing this book to put into words the ideas I had concerning the numerous factors involved in creating the person we become. This interest began when, as a teenager, I could not understand how unbelievably different my four brothers and I were. We were five different peas in the same pod. It didn't make sense: same parents, same happy home environment, but vastly different children.

What began as a search for answers to my problems became a realisation that, not only do most people not think about such things but, even if they wanted to, there were no guidelines as to how to go about it (this was in the days before the Internet). It was like wanting to study a subject, but unable to find a teacher or suitable reading material.

I came to the conclusion that the process existing for

understanding or aiding personal development could be likened to being put into a lifeboat at birth and cast upon the oceans of life. If fortunate, we encounter friendly currents and helpful winds. If not, but face storms or enter dangerous waters, we have to teach ourselves to navigate. Where life is concerned, too many of us are just left to get on with it, drifting, unaware of our strengths, weaknesses, or potential.

I was lucky. I had a huge incentive to discover what makes each of us tick. I wanted to know the origins of the many variables that went into making my brothers and me so different. Over time, I came to realise that this interest was also helping me to understand myself and to be more tolerant of those around me.

I had no idea where the task would take me, and am still amazed at some of the conclusions I came to along the way.

This book has evolved into a form of introduction to the origins of human behaviour—a book for examining some of the magic and mysteries involved in making you and me the persons we became.

My role is to provide and to examine relevant matters. I am essentially providing more questions than answers. I am suggesting which ways to go, not what you will find. I am suggesting what available evidence there is for you to take into consideration, including some of my own ideas, and it is up to you to agree or disagree with me.

You must decide whether or not this book encourages you to become interested in the subject of our origins, and to decide what you are going to do about it.

Why begin by looking at so much animal behaviour?

The beauty of examining the behaviour of species that have existed for many millions of years is the confidence we have that what we discover is how Nature determined it should be.

In their natural habitats, chosen to meet the needs of the species, they have evolved to live in harmony with their surroundings, be it on or below the ground, in the sea, or in the air. Unlike humans, it cannot be claimed that their behaviour and development have been moulded by such external influences as poverty, poor housing, racism, or inadequate educational and job opportunities. We can be quietly confident that their character and behaviour is the window that displays the complete package of personal qualities they possessed at birth and which were, to some extent, influenced by their environment.

This confidence enabled me to form opinions and draw conclusions about the origins of their behaviour—in particular, which aspects were purely instinctive and which were more "personal." After all, what surfaced in their evolution could have carried on into ours.

Instinctive behaviour

For me, the principal fascination of *instinct* is that it proves the genetic capability in all species to pass on knowledge and abilities to future generations.

If it had already been proved beyond doubt that humans possessed instinctive behaviour and abilities, including the gift of *inherited memories*, we would have been amazed to discover that comparatively primitive species, with infinitely less brainpower, also possessed a similar gift. We might even have been distinctly disappointed that something we treasured in our species was clearly and abundantly available in the most primitive of species.

A further benefit in studying animal behaviour was to discover the surprising *diversity* of "instinct."

Humans have been brought up to believe that instincts were

something that animals were born with to enable them to survive as a species. The spider's web is the perfect example of this. The web is the spider's home and provider of food. Without that gift, the spider could not survive.

But there are plenty of examples of "instincts" that are not necessarily "tools for survival."

The male weaver bird has the innate ability to build an intricate, hanging nest, yet this need not have been a prerequisite for the survival of the species. Other types of nest could well have served the purpose but, over time, the intricate hanging nest became the type that the females came to accept as the safest and most efficient, and it became the defining mate selection item. Consequently, capable nest-building skills eventually became an "instinct." This tells us, over time, that a "preferred choice" can develop into an instinct. Different species of birds instinctively build their own types of nest in specific locations. Such instincts gradually evolved as being the most effective for them.

Mating displays are another example. We might expect that primitive animals possessing the biological urge to mate would find a member of the other gender and satisfy their needs. After all, the males all look alike, as do the females. Instead, we discover that, in numerous species, the female is extremely choosy in selecting her mate. While the males are all hot and bothered about it, the females know which qualities they require in a mate and can be extremely selective. Presumably, it was over a period of time, that the females came to indicate which quality inspired them to choose a particular mate, and that later evolved as an instinct. So, mating instincts may assist in the selection process, but they are certainly not essential for survival of the species.

We also discover that instinctive behaviour is not written in stone for all members of a species. Some animals are not born with a strong enough instinct. Consequently, their behaviour does not exactly follow the norm for the species.

When we watch television footage of newly-born turtles, we see them struggling upwards to escape their sandy nest, with the majority "instinctively" heading for the safety of the sea. Some appear disoriented and head out in all directions and are quickly snatched up by predators.

The generally accepted principle of animals mating, producing, and nurturing the next generation to ensure the survival of the species takes a blow when we realise that some animals completely reject this opportunity—be it European cuckoos or ducks laying their eggs in others' nests, mothers neglecting and rejecting their young, or animals that are not sexually interested in the opposite gender. The so-called maternal and parental *instinct* is far from perfect for many animals in all species.

There is even doubt as to whether it is instinctive. A case could be made that maternal and parental behaviour is closer to natural than instinctive. The stages from the biological need to mating, and the inevitable consequences that follow, must have been in the make-up of the species originally, before they came to be classed as instinctive.

Observing such differences in animal behaviour mirrors what we see in humans. If we would rather carry on working than raising a family, or are not maternal in nature, if we walk away from our responsibilities, or if we lean towards criminal activities, these are not the accepted norms for our society. Should we blame our character "differences" on our upbringing or our personal mental inheritance, inclinations, and choices?

Instinctive and Inherited Behaviour.
Is there a difference?

This may, at first, strike you as an unnecessary question, but there is a difference. Whereas instinctive behaviour is always inherited, and is *common to all members of a species*, inherited personal qualities, which are not possessed by all, will not be scientifically classed as instincts.

We use expressions such as a *"natural leader"* or a *"born leader."* It could be argued that, as some particular abilities come naturally to an individual, they could almost be classed as "instinctive" in that it is a *personal predisposition* to be or act in a certain way. The latter, I believe, can also be influenced by the individual and the environment, because humans have "choice" as a tool.

Sexuality

In what many would deem a perfect world, the sexual orientation of both genders would be heterosexual. This would have been the most efficient method of ensuring the continuation of a species.

But sexual orientation could not be further away from being *instinctive*, in the true sense of the word. As there is not a single orientation common to all members of the species. In fact, it is a perfect example of evolution being effective, but imperfect.

The spectrum of sexuality throughout the animal kingdom, which ranges from heterosexual, bisexual, and homosexual, may be described by some as disturbing or appalling, but what it cannot be called is *unnatural.*

No one can accuse members of primitive species of *choosing* their sexuality. Even to consider such a thought would be endowing them with powers of intelligence and choice they could not possibly possess. An individual animal's sexual preference is personally endowed and perfectly *natural*. This is indisputable.

A similar assessment of human sexuality encounters firm to violent opposition. Despite the evidence displayed by all other species, there are millions of people today who believe there is only one true human sexual orientation. They insist that heterosexuality is the only *acceptable* orientation in our species, and that all others are "deviations."

Furthermore, they insist that all practising deviants cast off their sexuality and revert to being heterosexuals. They could not be more ridiculous or display their ignorance more clearly if they were to stand on Speakers' Corner in Hyde Park, London, and proclaim that all black people were to revert to being white, or suffer the consequences.

The diversity of sexual orientation has been shown to exist in more than fifteen hundred species studied, and it has been prevalent from the beginning of time. It is simply a natural consequence of genetic inheritance and random selection.

Bisexuals can choose and change their sexual preference at any time because they find both genders attractive and are able to be sexually satisfied with both.

Research to explain the enigma of different sexualities has proved that it is not the result of hormonal differences. All males and females fall within the same hormonal parameters for their gender. Research to discover a *"sex gene"* in our DNA has revealed nothing. The answer must lie elsewhere.

If we are born with our sexual inclination, and hormones or gene abnormalities are ruled out, what explanation is there for such diversity?

If we consider the issue calmly and objectively, we can state that *sexual urges* are the same in all orientations, whereas *sexual arousal* requires a ***mental stimulus***. I therefore suggest that sexuality has a mental, not a physical, base. *"Beauty lies in the eye of the beholder."* The vehicle for mental stimulation and sexual arousal is the eye. *Visual attraction that results in sexual arousal determines sexual orientation.*

If sexual arousal is derived from looking at members of the other gender, you are heterosexual.

If your eyes tell you that members of the same gender are sexually stimulating, you have been born gay.

If you find both genders can be sexually enticing, you are bisexual.

This is no more surprising a revelation than declaring that some men are visually attracted to blondes with big breasts, while others prefer red heads with shapely legs.

If you are trying to come to terms with such a simplistic explanation to a sexuality conundrum, remember that, throughout the whole of your lineage, half of the contributors have been of the opposite gender to your own. It would not be rocket science to assume that some *"other gender"* influences found their way into each of our genetic packages. Some men find themselves with more feminine mannerisms and sensitivities, enjoying wearing silk clothes next to their skin, and so on.

Individual qualities

Fathoming out how we acquired our personal qualities is yet another question. Are they due to life's experiences or is there another influence?

Analysing animal behaviour was a good starting point. We know from close contact with domesticated animals that they can have plenty of character. Although species may have some collective behaviour, varying personal qualities and temperaments exist in individuals. One can only guess at which point the *individualism* in evolving species became natural, but there is no doubt it exists.

Domestic animals display individual character, temperament, and personality. It is easy for us to accept this principle with cats, dogs, and horses because we have lived and inter-reacted with them for thousands of years. It may not be so easy to accept individualism in ants, termites, and bees. We may find it amusing and acceptable in a cartoon film, but it requires a leap of faith to look down at a line of ants and think of them as "individuals."

Humans are not the first species to possess personal and emotional characteristics. Other species also have them in abundance. Because their mental capacity is different to ours, we are confident that they did not choose their qualities. They were born with them. It is difficult to imagine an animal of any size *deciding to be* timid or aggressive, brave or cowardly, or whether to be loving or selfish. One must conclude that what they are is how they were born. Would they be concerned about any personal deficiencies, such as lacking maternal instincts or leadership qualities? One has to doubt it.

When I was thinking and writing about them, I found myself looking on them as communities of individuals, admiring their work ethic and their achievements over millions of years.

Pre-human species have much to be thankful for. They live in harmony with their surroundings, grateful when there is food, water, safety, and companionship. Their brain allows them to be grateful for life and the enjoyment of the essentials of living. Most humans only reach that state of nirvana after being close to death, or after surviving drought and famine.

Human Behaviour

Understandably, during our evolutionary progress and with our superior brains, we have created *new* personal human qualities and taken some existing ones to new levels. These must have included such gems as *guilt, envy, ambition, feelings of superiority, condemnation, racism, genocide, and* the most influential of all, *the need to believe in an afterlife.*

We have also been brought up to believe that who we are and how we behave is mainly the outcome of what has happened to us since we were born. Did we have two parents during childhood? Were there siblings? How were we brought up and taught? Were we rich or poor? Was religion part of our upbringing? Did we have job opportunities, personal relationships, marriage, rearing children, facing success or failure? Throw these and many other variables into the human cake mix, and then out we pop, for better or worse, ranging from perfect to imperfect mature human beings.

Psychologists investigate every aspect of our upbringing to find explanations for our mental state and behaviour. Unfortunately, I have no personal experience of undergoing detailed psychological assistance for mental or behavioural difficulties, but I am under the impression that the first areas for investigation are physical or sexual abuse, disjointed family life, i.e., lack of opportunities of any kind—in other words, external influences. And when any are considered significant, they are latched on to explain our "deficiencies" as individuals and as members of society.

I am inclined to believe that, in more cases than we might suspect, our mental problems and our ability to deal with them are as much due to *who we are* (our *genetic core*) as to the never-ending impact of our life's experiences.

Frailties of the mind

Throughout the book, I refer to how little we understand the workings of the human mind. Scientists seem to be pinning their hopes on brain scans and gene analysis to help them gain a clearer picture. This approach is logical with the aid of developing technology, but progress continues to be frustratingly slow and, in some cases, almost non-existent.

In the chapter on **dreaming (Chapter 5)**, I express concern at how one's subconscious entity seems to take control while we sleep. This subconscious "controller," with ready access to all the neurons, nerve ends, and circuits in our brains, assumes the role of writer and film director for the night. These nightly "productions" range from being harmless or titillating, but some can be disturbing or extremely unpleasant for the sleeper.

I can't recall reading of other people being as concerned as I am at the possible significance of this subconscious control. Dreams seem to be accepted as a form of *"release"* of tension, stress, desires, and fears that exist in our conscious mind. They are considered a natural release valve during sleeping hours and are supposed to be telling us something about ourselves.

I can understand this point of view, but I feel this explanation is only part of the truth.

The subconscious mind also *creates* unpleasant scenarios that cause stress and fear that become such regular occurrences for some people that they dread falling asleep. How is the subconscious releasing tensions and fears by doing this?

What is the purpose of silly dreams or "stupid" dreams that bemuse us or make us feel that *"someone"* is playing practical jokes (or worse) with our minds, and has our life's memories to play with. And they don't have to be recent.

Over forty years ago, one of my brothers went to work early to repair a machine in a factory. He was concentrating on this when someone arrived and switched on the electricity. The machines were activated and the result was my brother lost his arm. He has been dead many years, and I have not thought about that incident for a long time.

Recently, I dreamt that I was fixing a machine and someone switched on the main power. The machine cut off my hand. I woke up and was amazed to see my hand intact.

My point in telling that is to explain in part why I have concerns about the power of the subconscious. It has the power and the ability to play with the archives of our minds.

Whatever the subconscious mind is, it is definitely capable of playing games with our dreams. It evidently enjoys being in control. Fortunately, when dreams become too disturbing or frightening, we can escape them by waking up. This is our only true release or defense mechanism during the night.

If we had a choice, many of us would wish to have dreamless nights. But the choice is not ours. This tells us it is not possible for our "conscious mind" to be in control at night.

The situation we have to accept is that there is a *conscious* controller (supposedly ourselves) while we are aware and awake, and a *subconscious* controller when we sleep.

What if our subconscious controller becomes stronger and more influential than our conscious one? Would that not lead to our nighttime director of dreams controlling our conscious mind during the day, but without our natural release of "waking up"? Would that not lead to dire consequences for some unfortunates?

Mental illness

Commenting on mental illness and its possible causes is not easy or wise for a layperson. It is such a major issue in our community that opinions from unqualified persons, such as myself will surely be dismissed out of hand with the question,

"Where is your proof?" or more likely, *"What are your qualifi-cations?"* And that is how it should be.

This stumbling block has never stopped us from expressing opinions in the past and I am sure it won't in the future.

I have expressed opinions in this book because I feel that somewhere there may be a kernel of truth in them. My mind tells me that my ideas may be worth reading. Furthermore, they are included for lay people to consider, digest, and argue about. Mental illness still retains something of the "loony bin" image. Anything that moves people away from such conceptions cannot be all bad. There needs to be greater public awareness of mental health issues. To do this, they need to be supplied with information.

Could the subconscious contribute to mental illness?

Because the subconscious bears such influence while we are asleep, it begs the question about its potential influence during the day. Could it be harmful?

Dreams and hallucinations belong to the same family. Voices and images are conjured up in both. Why should we be ex-pected to accept uncontrolled nighttime dreams as a form of "release," but classify uncontrollable daytime "hallucinations and voices" as an illness? After all, the main distinction between them is that people have hallucinations only when they are awake and have no immediate means of escaping them. For those who feel they are losing their minds because they cannot exercise mental control during the day, they can only "dream" (no pun intended) of discovering the cause or cure.

Therapy may begin with questions as to their relationships, childhood, sexual abuse, and other mistreatment, all of which are external factors. If therapy is not working, more often than not, they will be given controlling drugs to suppress the symptoms. These drugs may then produce unpleasant side effects. The possibility of a cure is less than satisfactory, and there is a spiralling down effect of the treatment that, in serious cases, can eventually lead to suicide.

I feel there should be as much, if not more, emphasis first on discovering whether some causes of delusions come from within us. Depression begins in many young people in their teens, even when external factors do not appear to have had time to be the cause of them.

Treatment of mental illness

Although science and medicine will continue to make advances in the treatment of discernible, brain deterioration and diseases such as Parkinson's and Alzheimer's, curing mental illnesses is a far more nebulous and difficult challenge.

I had the temerity to include this section on the grounds that, if I should develop a mental illness, instead of being given therapy, anti-depressants, stronger drugs or ECT (electric treatment) to suppress the symptoms, I would request other treatment.

Initially, I would prefer to be hypnotised to establish whether the immediate causes of my condition were in my conscious or subconscious mind.

If this did not produce results, I would request to undergo *past-life regression* to ascertain whether my subconscious contained any disturbing mental issues passed on to me at birth. If all that failed, then I am sure I would be grateful for the benefit of modern drugs.

Multiple Personality Disorder (MPD)

My reasons for including a segment on this particular disorder were: I disagree that external traumas are always the primary **cause** of all the symptoms of a mental illness. I see them as essentially the *trigger for releasing* the transfer of disorder symptoms from the subconscious to the conscious. Attributing trauma as the **cause** of producing additional personalities in the subconscious does not seem logical, practicable, or believable to me.

Over the years, I became more and more convinced that we inherit far more mentally than we might think and, considering what amazing things the animal kingdom does regarding genetic transfer, I deemed it far more probable that the additional identities associated with MPD were present in the subconscious *before* the traumas. If this is the case, then it means we are all born with ancestral memories of additional "personalities"

Past-life therapy

For those of you who still smile at the mere idea of seeking details of "past-lives" under deep hypnosis, let me say that intelligent, qualified hypnotists, many belonging to the mental health profession, believe in it. "Past" or "Previous" Life Therapy are not descriptions I support because they both imply that what the person under deep hypnosis is describing are events in **their** previous lives. I think this is incorrect. I think they are *ancestral memories* describing people, places, and events that happened in the lives of some of their forebears. They inherited these memories and are accessing them under deep hypnosis. Accordingly, a better description of the therapy would be **Ancestral Memory Regression** and Ancestral Memory Therapy.

If the existence of ancestral identities and memories were given more serious consideration by the professionals, their potential influences on illnesses would be taken into account, and it could be assessed whether or not they are a source of such problems as hallucinations, hearing voices, additional identities, phobias, severe depression, or other symptoms.

Mental illness develops when external factors impact on the subconscious. Considering ancestral memory as a potential influence would lead to further study of the subconscious and the emergence of other identities. Because a hypothesis appears to contain flaws, it should not be casually dismissed as "unscientific."

Throughout history, *not having been acknowledged by the scientific community*" has been proved to be insufficient grounds to reject many a hypothesis.

Memories

In the chapter on Memories, I mentioned my hundred-year-old grandmother being able to recall childhood memories, yet unable to recogsize her own daughter. The mental chamber holding them had been protected from the mental ravages of old age. Who can positively deny the existence of an *Inherited Memories* chamber secreted in the subconscious? I am ready to believe it.

Individualism

Individualism is the word I use to describe a person's unique combination of human qualities—not merely the physical body, but personal and humanitarian qualities, including those honed by environmental influences, plus the inevitable mental inheritance of character, temperament, and emotional base. The combination of all these influences renders each of us as unique as our DNA.

Environmental influences on us as we mature nurture some elements of our being and cause others to wither. They test and probe us to reveal strengths and weaknesses, tempting us to follow one path or another, and giving us the chance to bloom or fade.

I believe most of us are born with the ability to do good and evil. I say this, not as a religious faith, but because I feel sure that is the nature of our innate random inclinations. Many of our personal strengths and weaknesses could be inherited. The big challenge is to discover what they are and to develop the right ones.

This does not mean that we are blessed or condemned by our lineage, but my view is that our mental inheritance can strongly influence who we become. Awareness of our physical and mental strengths and weaknesses should be an essential aid to growing to maturity. I have had to learn mine the hard way. If people had spoken to me honestly about my strengths and weaknesses (as they saw them) when I was younger, I would have paid far more attention to who I was and who I wanted to become much sooner in life.

It has taken me many decades to do that and I had to write a book to begin to sort it out in my mind. The youth of today cannot wait that long. They need better guidance than they are receiving. I see the society of today, even more than in the past, allowing and almost encouraging them to *drift* into maturity, treating them as if they are supposed to be mature when they are young. I think *I* drifted, and I lived in the times of strict school discipline and National Service. The youth of today do not even have those markers to help them.

Society must do what is best for the development of young people, not what it thinks might be best for the feelings of society. More than ever, the youth of today need a helping hand. More effective methods than exist at present have to be examined, tried, and tested.

I strongly believe that, as our physical body reflects our lineage, so do our mental strengths and weaknesses. The title of this book, was originally **Polished Diamonds,** because it recognised how we all arrive as rough diamonds whose edges are gradually rounded by contact with environmental influences throughout our lives, but our *core being* will always be the original diamond we were at birth. Whether any flaws contained therein are permanent or unmanageable is really one for the scientists.

I eventually changed it to **The Origins of Human Behaviour** when I came to realise that the **origins** were much more important than the behaviour. If we could understand them, we should be able to understand ourselves in a more constructive way.

I would love there to be courses in schools that covered the variables involved in **Human Behaviour**. It should be possible. After all, they have started sex education. Young people should also learn the dynamics behind such qualities as bullying, tolerance, shyness, hatred, personal development, and individual potential. Something is needed to counter the insensitive cruelty latent in children.

How I would love there to be a controlled experiment to reveal more guidelines on the major influences in our lives.

I would set up a control group consisting of one hundred children raised with all the advantages of life and a hundred children from deprived areas.

Then, I would take a hundred children from deprived areas and have them raised with all the advantages of life, and transfer one hundred advantaged children to be raised in a more deprived environment. The trial would be to assess the resulting behaviour of the "saints and sinners" in both control groups with those of the children who were moved from one lifestyle to the other.

Would the originally rich children contain significantly more *"prison fodder"* due to their deprived upbringing, and would the deprived children produce more *"good citizens"* than found in the control group? What a delightful proposition.

Such an experiment would never be allowed in a democratic society, but if it were, would the major influences prove to be **Nature** (inherited) or **Nurture** (environmental)?

What do you think?

PART FOUR –
OUR PERSONAL DEVELOPMENT

Part Four explains how an understanding of the origins of
human behaviour enables us to become more involved in
the personal development of ourselves and our loved ones.

The Realisation

It was during the writing of this book that I realised I had never considered playing any active role in my own personal development. Oh, I had been heavily involved in playing sports and other activities in school, and planning about doing things at university and in the army, but I cannot recall ever consciously assessing **me** and the person I was.

My childhood and teenage years had rushed by into becoming a young, then mature person until now, in my seventies, I have concluded that I simply *evolved* into being me. In an earlier chapter I described the process as having *'evolved in my own little bubble.'*

Is that what most of us do? Do we just grow up without consciously thinking about ourselves and, even worse, grow old without attempting to do anything positive about who we become?

Must we live with ourselves, meekly accepting our pluses and minuses, as if adopting the philosophical view of *"That's life"*?

I have an overwhelming feeling this is utterly wrong. Animals may be unable to influence who they become, but we, with our superior brains, should be able to.

This section of the book sets out to explain that *drifting* into maturity and old age is not how it has to be, and it examines how and why we should at least consider playing a more thoughtful and positive role in the determination of the person we become.

Unfortunately, as with so many other things in our lives, there seems to be no external encouragement or direction to believe such things are possible. Perhaps now is the time for change. If we can introduce an expansion and development of our mental awareness and understanding, we and our species would benefit.

That sounds pretentious, doesn't it? *"Expanding and developing the mental awareness of the species."* After all, improving one's mental awareness could never be as easy as having cosmetic surgery to improve one's physical appearance.

The significant goal is *awareness*. We have been allowing ourselves and our children to *evolve* into people because we have been **unaware** we could be more actively involved in the process. I am not advocating a *"How to be a better person"* campaign. I want us to have a greater **understanding**, not only of the mechanics of human behaviour; but of the potential sources of our qualities and emotions. Armed with such knowledge, we would not feel obliged to *drift* into being ourselves but would have the knowledge and the confidence, if we should be so inclined, to think more about ourselves and to consider attempting a more structured involvement in the challenge of becoming a unique human being.

You may disagree with this and feel there is already plenty of positive input into personal development via the home, school, church and elsewhere. Certainly, there is plenty of instruction as to what to do, when and how to do it. But that is all input about **what to do**. The awareness I am referring to deals with thinking about **who to be**.

In everything we do, there is that interaction between what we do and why we do it. For example, one person donating time and money supporting charities will do so for commendable reasons, while another's aim might be to obtain a knighthood. *What* one does is seen by the world, *why* one does it is entirely personal. Others can judge us by what we do. We should be judging ourselves by why we do things.

You may already be convinced we are not able to influence our personal development. This would not be all that surprising if you have accepted the view that *"Life's experiences are the prime factors influencing our personal development"*. You may be inclined to agree that we do *"evolve in the great bubble that is the world around us"*.

This claim of life's experiences being the most influential factor in personal development precludes the possibility of there being other significant influences and implies there is no need for the individual to search for other sources. This may appear reasonable, because we know certain experiences can impact on our lives, but it is still a flawed premise.

For example, take the students at any famous public school in England. They will have come from very well off or rich family backgrounds, and experienced a comfortable upbringing which, on purely environmental grounds, should have helped them to develop into the ***"best that humanity can become"***. They may present a similar façade, looking and behaving like a so-called elite segment of society but, if we were to delve into the 'personal qualities' of each and every individual, we would discover they had as equal a share of personal *pluses and minuses* as any group from a deprived area.

If I am to advocate that major aspects of our personal make-up, such as temperament, character and personality, are not simply the product of life's experiences, then I have to present alternative sources. Such 'sources' need to be identified, examined and analysed to convince you they are worthy of your serious consideration.

Accepting Our Evolutionary Inheritance

Before introducing alternative sources for personal development in humans, we need to recall information covered earlier in the book.

If we accept the theories expounded in Darwin's *Origin of the Species*, we know our species owes a great debt to countless others that evolved before us. Their successes contributed to making our species a reality, because we are all part of the same tree of life.

It is logical to conclude that facets of behaviour, which evolved over millions of years, would be carried forward into later species. This is the whole basis of an evolutionary process. One would not expect a new species to evolve independently without identifiable qualities present in earlier species.

In **Part 1**, important aspects of animal behaviour were examined in some detail because it was felt that what worked for other species could well be working for us.

Many species have developed mental gifts so amazing that the brightest human minds still cannot explain them. Scientists gave them a generic word *'instinct'*.

Humans have become mesmerised by the link between instinct and animal behaviour. We have been told so much about the *instinctive (unthinking) behaviour* in animals that we could be forgiven for believing that many species, seemingly less intelligent than our own, possess a clone mentality leading to considerable instinctive and unthinking behaviour.

I am sure that nothing could be further from the truth. Anyone who owns animals or worked with them, domesticated or wild, would claim they have their individual character, temperament and personality. We know that individual animals can be dominant or submissive, good or bad mothers, friendly or aggressive, and so on. If you were asked for an opinion as to the origin of their individual personal qualities, would you assume they were moulded by their environment, or would you think it more likely **they were born with them?**

If the latter is true, it would mean they are born possessing both the *instincts of the species* and other distinctive *personal qualities*. There is every reason to believe this is the norm in the animal kingdom because the individuals do not have the time, knowledge, intelligence or ability to consider, select and develop personal characteristics. They do not have to choose whether they will be dominant or submissive, gentle or aggressive. Their individual qualities do not come from the species but from their *direct lineage*.

Indeed, modern animal breeding practices are based on the principle that both physical and mental qualities can be genetically transferred to progeny.

Homo sapiens

Our species appeared approximately two hundred thousand years ago. (*Not a long period when compared to numerous other species that have existed for more than two hundred million years.*)

It is generally accepted that humans do not need so-called

survival instincts because we are nurtured from cradle to grave. It is also said that our character, temperament and other personal qualities are acquired and developed as a result of our exposure to life's experiences. Some also claim that, at birth, the human mind is a clean slate waiting to be written on by external events.

The claim that environmental influences mould us into human beings completely ignores the evidence provided by countless earlier species. Not only does the animal kingdom give abundant proof that instincts are passed on to future generations, it also reveals how individual animals are born with mental qualities and emotional levels derived from their lineage.

We are acknowledged as being part of the animal kingdom. There are even unnecessary parts of our body that are remnants from our evolutionary past. The DNA levels of other species can reach up to ninety-eight percent of our own. Our physical shape is that of our species, but our personal physical features are strongly influenced by our lineage.

Why would our species be the first not to have our minds *influenced by our ancestral line?*

Perhaps the argument is that we are such an intelligent and advanced species we do not need to inherit them. Which processes determined that is how it should be? Evolution carries on without a committee deciding whether or not we would be too intelligent to need ancestral assistance. We *evolved* as a species. There was no cancellation of lineage physical links, so what scientific proof is there that ancestral, mental influences were deleted from our evolutionary development?

I would think that, with our dramatically enhanced brain potential, it was more likely that our ancestral mental *links would be enhanced rather than reduced.*

The fact that some people do not believe inherited mental 'features' are a significant factor in our development means little without scientific proof. After all, when we are told we currently use only ten percent of our brain capacity, should that fact not encourage us to wonder what mysteries await to be discovered in the remaining ninety percent?

Ancestral Influences on the Human Mind 32

Whereas lineage physical characteristics are visible and recognisable, ancestral mental influences in the subconscious are neither transparent nor readily identifiable.

I consider *mental influences* to be temperament and character traits, emotional tendencies and predispositions towards such qualities as being dominant, determined, ambitious, shy or gregarious, etc.

I believe this because human behaviour suggests that one's actions and attitudes owe much to genetic origin. Examples may not be as spectacular as the Monarch butterfly's transfer of all information required for a five month migration covering three thousand miles, but they are still worthy of note.

The genetic transfer of knowledge, skills, attitudes and information which leads to specific behaviour in *all* member of a species is known as **Instinct**. Genetic transfer of *personal qualities* (received by progeny of a direct line) is an *ancestral package* sourced from the animal's direct lineage.

Although it is easier to accept that genetic mental transfer exists in the animal kingdom, many people are less willing to acknowledge that such an ancestral package plays a significant role in human mental activity.

What works for others in the animal kingdom should work for us. We are told that our mind employs a process of neurons and neural circuitry to interpret, store and access information and memories. It is reasonable to assume that the minds of other species possess a similar ability which they use not only to transfer instinctive knowledge to progeny, such as details of migrations, nest and web building, but also to pass on emotional packages such as parental devotion or lack of it (cuckoo). Even the natural avian fear of humans can be bypassed in the robin. The animal kingdom could not survive in its present state without effective mental transfer of knowledge and personal qualities.

Evidence supporting genetic mental transfer in humans.

I know that much of who I am must have come from within me because I did not try to be a specific person and do not recall my parents or teachers telling what sort of person to be, yet I reached university at the end of my 'teens and I was "me". I had an ordinary, uneventful upbringing and yet, with little effort on my part, and without being ambushed by any dramatic, external influences, I became a unique human being. That in itself is not a decisive argument, even for me, but my awareness of that fact prompted a need for further explanations.

Members of a large family can be amazed at the different characters, temperaments, personalities and interests of their siblings. They may wonder how their mother and father, with their own particular qualities, managed to produce such a diverse group, with so many identities and personalities present in the same household!

Assuming we are beginning to accept the possibility of this

nebulous idea of an 'ancestral package' in each of us, what other factual evidence is available?

Personal Qualities

The personal qualities you possess combine to make you a unique individual. The interesting question is how you came to acquire them.

Think about what you would consider to be your best personal traits. Are you of good character, emotionally stable, reasonably independent, caring but ambitious, confident and kind, hard-working and reliable, unselfish and loving? Those are just a few of the good ones. Think how many bad qualities there are!

Most personality traits have a *plus* and a *minus* side, such as honest/dishonest, generous/mean, hard-working/lazy etc. The range of qualities is quite mind-blowing. (A list of some of them was given in **Chapter 21**).

The mystery surrounding them is that no one knows how and why they develop within us. If someone treats us brutally, will we become timid or a bad-tempered bully? If we are treated with kindness, would that help us to develop a pleasant and kind nature, or would we learn to take advantage of it? If we are constantly confronted by lies and deceit, do we become more honest or more deceitful?

The conundrum is whether the *'influences'* make us who we are, or whether *who we already are* helps us to deal with the influences?

If you have glanced at the list of qualities in **Chapter 21**, you might begin wondering what kind of life's experiences might cause you to develop some of them because, amazing though it may seem, all those qualities are part of your personal make-up to some extent, even when they are negatives (i.e. **not** selfish).

Could it really be possible we acquire them as we go through life facing all sorts of situations, problems and other environmental influences?

The weakness of such a theory is it fails to explain how young people, brought up encountering similar environmental influences, be they good or bad, can develop completely different 'packages' of personal qualities. Indeed, the differences can be so significant that people from the same background can range in nature from psychopath to saint.

External factors may influence some personal qualities, but they do not create them. Our spectrum of good and bad personal qualities is so great that we have to seek elsewhere for an explanation of their origin and diversity.

Additional Identities and Personalities

When I discussed the problems of sufferers of MPD (Multiple Personality Disorder) in **Chapter 20**, I said I was unable to accept the theory that their multiple identities/personalities were created as a by-product of traumatic physical and sexual abuse.

While agreeing that the subconscious mind is creative, I find it hard to accept it is able to create and retain additional and unique identities as a result of **external** abuse. If I am justified in taking this view, the most likely explanation for their creation must be that they originate from **internal** sources.

If this is so, for a subconscious to be able to secrete such a range of individual and extremely varied personalities, the most likely source has to be *genetic*. When these 'identities' surface in an MPD sufferer they can be numerous (the average is eight, but it can be scores), male or female, different sexualities, different age groups, dominant or submissive: in other words, a **cross-section of humanity.**

It is difficult to imagine a single subconscious creating such a plethora of diverse identities under any circumstances. What other source could it draw upon?

It is more logical to consider that such personalities are derived, in some shape or form, from ancestral identities or memories.

You may consider this explanation to be somewhat alarming: *ancestral identities* in the subconscious? **How** could such a genetic phenomenon be possible and, even more important, **why** would it to be necessary?

The 'how' is readily explained. We already know that so-called additional identities can exist in the human subconscious. The animal kingdom also clearly demonstrates that genetic transfer of personal qualities to progeny is natural or, put another way, **the genetic transfer of different identities for individual animals** in a species is a reality. It is also possible for parents to produce progeny with qualities *they do not display themselves*.

This could also be said of humans. My identity and those of my siblings certainly did not replicate those of our parents, just as I am sure the minds of a psychopathic killer or potential saint could be worlds apart from the identities of their parents.

Perhaps describing the process as *the transfer of 'identities' or 'personalities'* is misleading because it is using well-known, descriptive words to describe an unknown process. They are inadequate words because they appear to imply that complete ancestral *identities* and *personalities* are being genetically transferred. I cannot say whether or not this is the case. I am using the words to encapsulate the magical transfer of a random selection of mental qualities which may well become the cornerstone of the individual's 'individuality' and which, under certain circumstances, can be drawn upon by the subconscious for the formation of personal traits, additional identities or personalities.

This genetic transfer, in whatever shape or form, is our inherited **genetic core** which could well supply our multitudinous personal qualities, memories, other identities, hallucinations, nightmares and other mental malfunctions. It could also serve as the ancestral pool of numerous human qualities and personal inclinations, memories and areas of expertise. All such things are contained in the mind, and it is logical to deduce that a **core** consisting of innumerable and varied mental influences had to originate from a source of mental influences. If that source is internal, it must be ancestral in nature.

Each female egg and conquering male sperm contains their ancestral content and, when they join, they become a combined ancestral package.

You have now reached the point in the story where you have to consider whether my explanation of the origin of "additional identities" is just an airy-fairy concoction of hypothetical, circumstantial loose ends, or agree it could be a more logical and believable extrapolation of available facts than an unsubstantiated theory that severe sexual and physical abuse create numerous and varied additional identities in the subconscious.

If you are inclined to agree with me, or are still making up your mind, read on to discover why I believe the **ancestral core** phenomenon was an evolutionary necessity.

Why Have Additional Identities?

If additional 'identities' are ever-present in our subconscious, there has to be a sound evolutionary reason for it. They cannot exist simply as a species' aberration which has become a means for tormenting the mentally ill.

The whole concept is bewildering and, if we begin to associate it more broadly with mental illness, a little frightening. If they do exist in all of us as a natural phenomenon, we need to understand why, and be comfortable about their existence and purpose.

Planting a specific instinct into the mind of every member of a species must be reasonably straightforward. It is a *"species memory"* passed on to all members of the species.

If endowing individual animals with personal qualities were to be attempted using a similar process, a species would consist of cloned members having the same instinctive behaviour patterns and personal qualities.

At some point, evolutionary processes determined that individuals in a species need not be cloned, allowing some to be dominant or submissive, timid or vicious, selfish or unselfish, good or poor parents, and so on. It was also a means of constantly improving the species. Such an innovation required a separate biological process, and the convenient and natural source for providing such a varied range of qualities was via direct lineage.

Selecting and transferring to the next generation a concoction of personal qualities from two long and varied ancestral lines has to be a far more complex procedure than transmitting a single species memory.

Let us assume we humans do receive a physical and mental 'endowment' at birth. Our physical traits are so clearly laid down that we require surgery to change them, but our 'personal nature' has to be more flexible, otherwise we would all be "blessed or condemned" by what was in our ancestral package.

Personal mental qualities seem to evolve gradually from within us as we mature. Interestingly, young people can go through various mental phases such as angelic child, unsettled youngster, infuriating teenager and then over-confident university student, all with unconscious ease. Each phase may be supported by additional input from the ancestral core, as part of the evolving process. Fortunately, the various maturing phases mentioned above do not produce the same results for all young people. Some parents are much luckier than others.

If the development of a person is linked to attitude and behavioural changes periodically, and if the unique character and nature of the individual is being formed, there has to be a source supplying them. I have described the source as our 'ancestral core', but I am of the opinion that the core includes ancestral identities. A similar process would also be the source of natural and individual personal qualities found in other species.

Although the concept of an *ancestral core made up of separate identities* may be difficult to accept, it still explains their presence in the subconscious, both for us and for other species.

Let us return to the example of a large family. The parents have their individual ancestral lines which have been accessed at each conception. The physical appearance of the children may be similar to that of a parent, grandparent or great grandparent, but the personal qualities of each child can be completely disparate, which would suggest their origins come from an even broader base. Even in families with only two or three children, there can be significant differences in the nature of the siblings. This random selection would appear to be the norm.

Please remember that such terms as *ancestral core*, *ancestral pool* and *identities* are figurative words used to describe a mystical process within us, just as *instinct* is an inadequate word used by all to describe certain mystical behaviour in animals.

The importance of inherited identities is for the mind to possess a source for releasing a myriad of personal qualities. There will be a random element involved in the selection of the qualities but the origins will be ancestral. As with all random selection processes, selection may include predispositions to be particularly sporty or artistic, full of confidence or shy, kind or cruel.

Influencing Who We Become

Having reached the stage of accepting that additional identities could be of internal origin, and having come to terms with the concept that multiple 'identities' could be the means of creating a pool of personal traits in our subconscious, a number of further issues need clarifying.

We need to be convinced that our personal traits are so numerous and complex that they must be more flexible in nature than our physical traits, otherwise the sort of person we are would be as unchangeable as our physical appearance.

External factors could influence the accessing of qualities from the ancestral pool. I have already given the example of the Church or State encouraging individuals to carry out inhuman acts against others without any official retribution. Some may refuse to do so (possibly with serious personal consequences), others may do it reluctantly with feelings of guilt, while there will always be some who discover they enjoy the feelings of power and domination when carrying out such acts.

This process is not one of external forces **moulding** a person's character, but of them serving to discover whether or not particular character traits are present within a person's ancestral core. This is an important difference which helps to explain the different development of people in any environment, good or bad.

When a person is confronted by a completely new situation requiring a specific response, one can imagine the individual subconsciously accessing the 'ancestral pool' to help them deal with the problem. It may be the first time a friend is encouraging them to steal, or in a war situation when rescuing a colleague would mean putting one's own life at risk. The core is accessed and the decision is taken. Such moments determine whether or not that person is capable of being a thief or a hero.

If access and changes can be made in emergency situations, alterations should be possible by personal choice in less stressful situations.

This can be achieved less dramatically at a different level by exposing individuals to various activities which may or may not provide them with pleasure and quality time. Schools provide such opportunities by exposing pupils to studying, public speaking, acting, choral singing, sports and athletics.

I can still remember my art teacher giving the class, *An Aspect of Nature,* for homework. I painted something that was supposed to be a daffodil. The boy sitting alongside me had painted a landscape with rolling fields, hedgerows, copses with a hint of humans and animals. I was absolutely amazed at the differences in our natural talents. His had bloomed, mine didn't even bud. I came to the same conclusion in woodwork after I had spent almost two years trying unsuccessfully to make a simple wooden object. I now know that such interests and skills were not in my ancestral package then or since.

Similarly, no matter how much encouragement the 'environment' offers in developing self-confidence, some of us will avoid public speaking or acting at any cost. On the other hand, those who possess the flame of wanting to act, even those suffering badly from nerves, will brush aside all obstacles to achieve their dream.

None of my numerous siblings took music lessons yet one brother taught himself to play the piano 'by ear'. He could churn out any of the popular melodies of the day. His gift of musicality must have been so strong that he did not need external influences to develop it. His talent surfaced of its own accord. No one else in the family touched the piano. I could imagine this happening to those desperate to paint or dance, while others without specific talents might *want to be famous*. They possess an inner driving force, similar to that of the salmon desperately seeking to reach its river of origin.

But school also exposes pupils to discipline, a work ethic and interaction with others. Most pupils will respond positively and enjoy their years at school while the natural inclination of others will be to react in more negative ways and desperate to reject that phase of their lives. Such responses have nothing to do with intelligence.

If these ancestral identities serve as a *pool* of qualities to form the basis of our natural self, and if it can be accessed to discover we are able us to commit atrocities or acts of bravery and compassion, then we need to be confident we are able to access it for other personal changes. We need to understand that it is natural to have *pluses and minuses* in our nature. Our next concern should be whether we are able or wish to do anything about them.

Can We Change?

Hopefully, this book has encouraged you to think about yourself and who you are. Knowing more about the origins of behaviour and being aware there may be other qualities in your subconscious is all very well, but the big question is whether it will be of any use to you and the ones you love?

Part Four presents you with a series of ideas to demonstrate that there is a recognisable structure to who each one of us is. I hope I have shown that our uniqueness and individualism could be a natural, evolutionary phenomenon in which our minds are blessed with information derived from our ancestral line. The words used to describe the process are not as important as the concept.

We assume the 'pool' can be accessed but, in examples already given, it required special circumstances such as official permission to commit atrocities with impunity. Even so, positive responses to such demands can only be possible if the required 'qualities' are contained in one's ancestral package. There will be many, desperate to be brave, who will eventually come to accept that such a quality is not within them. There will be others, called upon to fight and kill, who will also be unable to find the commitment within them to do it.

How does one access "the Pool"?

The prerequisites for anyone contemplating making conscious changes to some aspects of their persona, however insignificant, must be an acceptance there are other qualities within them, and a willingness to give them the opportunity to surface.

Older people have been known to produce a list of the ten things they would *like to do* before they die, their *Bucket* List, and then tick them off as each one is completed.

Anyone can produce a list, however small, of personal traits they would like to remove or possess. The very fact of wanting the change is, in itself, a personal achievement. The determination to acquire it is an additional bonus, and applying oneself to the task is, in itself, significant.

For example, take a young person with no time for "useless, pathetic, old people", mocking them and throwing stones at their front door for fun. For whatever reason, he comes to realise that he is the pathetic figure, not the elderly persons he mocks, so he is persuaded to change. He tries to make it up to them by doing jobs about the house and helping them in other ways. He is surprised to discover 'the elderly couple' have had interesting lives, are nice people, and he ends up making new friends. He might even come to change his attitude to the elderly in general.

Some personal feelings and attitudes may have been part of our make-up for so long, only determination and persistent effort will lead to the desired results. Addictive behaviour is a perfect example of this. Whether it is giving up gambling, smoking, drinking or drugs, the conscious mind must want to stop the habit. There may be many reasons for wanting to control one's addiction: financial desperation, future of the family or personal health. One must use the most important one as the trigger for success, and keep trying.

Overcoming addictive behaviour of any kind requires conviction, strength of character, determination and application. No wonder it is difficult. The fact that you keep trying shows determination, and that many others in the same position as yourself have succeeded gives cause for hope. Your main problem is not kicking the habit; it is believing that at least one of the essential fighting qualities has to be in your ancestral package, be it determination, strength of character, love of family, belief in prayer or just sheer bloody-mindedness. Find it and use it as your platform to give you a chance of success. You could surprise yourself!

An easier goal might be deciding to change your natural inclination *'to put things off until a better time'*. You might have had a serious argument with an old friend or family member and stubbornly refused to contact them for years. Stubbornness and pride can be swept away with a word or a phone call, and your reward will be the additional pleasure of having them back in your life.

You might have been thinking for years about writing a book but 'never got round to doing it'. Don't worry about whether or not it will be published, just think of the potential pleasure and satisfaction to be derived from writing it.

How long have you put off discovering more about your family tree? Starting that journey might not only be a revelation for you, it would become of great interest to future generations.

Most of us would not want drastic changes, but there would be certain things about ourselves we might want to alter. Knowing that you have the means is a good start.

Who to be

I think the starting point in deciding how to change or **who to be** is to make an honest evaluation of **who you are**. This can be undertaken at any age, and it need not be done as a desperately serious enterprise.

Producing an honest assessment is not as easy as it sounds because we are rarely honest about our personal qualities (mainly because we never normally undertake such a responsible task).

In **Chapter 21** I included a large basic list of personal qualities as a template to help a person discover how others assessed them. That would be a useful, objective beginning, even if it did destroy some memorable relationships. (*Just kidding*)

Even parents assessing their own children can be reluctant to be entirely honest, because honesty often offends. Parents who try to draw attention to what they deem to be particular 'failings' in a child will not find the task easy or appreciated.

Is there a more workable approach?

The approach I would advocate for introducing this subject to young people would need various phases:

(1) I would want the children to understand and accept that personal qualities are not fixed items like a face or finger prints. They will most probably be happy to accept that animals are born with personal qualities, and from this they can move on to believing many personal qualities originate within us. If they can accept the existence of ancestral influences and realise these can be accessed, they may be willing to think about the subject. The effective beginning will be convincing themselves to **think about themselves** in a positive way.

(2) Mental professionals *have to agree* that individuals can

benefit from being made aware of the origins of human behaviour. (If not as portrayed in this book then at least as agreed by the professional community). They must decide to promote mental awareness in all its forms. They need to be worthy of the respect of the public.

(3) A generally agreed booklet of information could be produced to ensure uniformity in what was being expressed generally or in schools. Parents could purchase it to be aware of how the subject was being presented to their children.

(4) Schools would be the best environment for introducing the subject of behaviour and personal qualities. The benefits of this would be that pupils would not feel individually targeted (as they would at home) but, having had the origins of behaviour explained to them as a group, would then be able to discuss it freely amongst themselves. If the general consensus was that there "could be something in it", this would serve as a platform for tackling the subject further in school, at home or at an individual level, as and when warranted.

(5) When schools have done the groundwork, parents would feel more confident discussing the issue with their children and encouraging them to exchange ideas on the serious aspects of behaviour.

Traditional barriers to communication need to be tackled and removed. Young people must become confident that they are able to confide in their parents or teachers. Communication barriers lead to seriously damaged lives through bullying or sexual abuse. The fear of further abuse is harmful, but the dread of not being able to tell an adult about it brings utter helplessness. Such issues of behaviour need to be addressed immediately by all concerned.

We can all look back on our lives and assess how our parents failed us, or how we let our children down because of a failure to communicate. Countless people, particularly children, suffer because they have never been encouraged *"to talk about things"*. Paedophilia and other forms of sexual abuse flourish because of this failing. Children must be made aware that they are able to talk about what frightens and upsets them. That so many do not is a condemnation of our society's attitude to protecting them.

I started this journey of finding the origins of behaviour because I wanted to understand why I and my four brothers were so different, but it gradually expanded into wanting to understand people in general, and then myself and who I was. This then became a passion for wanting people to want to think more about the origins of behaviour, to benefit from thinking about themselves, and even encouraging them to seek guidance in mental matters which will enable them to help future generations.

We should ask ourselves whether the art of talking and discussing in the home is being strangled by television and the availability of numerous electronic gadgets for all ages. When this era of political over-correctness has come to an end, and the over-emotional attitudes towards so many things in our society have subsided, I can dream of an era containing harmonious and structured approaches to racism and homophobia, bullying, lying, gang culture, stealing, anti-social behaviour against the elderly, and so the list goes on. This is what the professionals should be offering us.

Who is responsible for our enlightenment?

Time will tell who is responsible, but any action will be an improvement on the present situation of appearing to allow young people to grow up without guidance, discipline or being made aware of their inner potential.

In fact, it could be said that parents and teachers, both essential to the personal development of young people, receive little guidance and information on how to assist children in the subject of growing up. Could the official view be that parents grew up themselves therefore they are qualified to be responsible for the development of others?

The time must come when a united mental profession will be pro-active in targeting the mental development of the young, including greater awareness of the potential frailties of the mind. Mental professionals should encourage them to think more about themselves and the likely sources of their individuality.

If we ever come to the point when we think we have lost confidence in government processes, the churches, the police and the future, we need to reinvent ourselves and the nation.

No matter what political and local government attempt to achieve, their efforts are likely to be criticised by many as "window dressing" or "vote catching".

This book sets out to suggest that you, **the reader**, should accept greater responsibility in wanting to learn more about how you came to be who you are. It pleads with you to place mental awareness much higher on your social agenda and to demand that you be given sufficient information on mental illness to be able to recognise early symptoms, to not be afraid of seeking early assistance and to empathise with sufferers of mental illness.

You could become the leaders of the public wanting to know more about what factors make us who we are. At the moment, lack of guidance could be turning us into directionless travellers.

At the beginning of the book, I referred to *Homo sapiens* having a brilliant brain and a fragile mind. I suspect a major contributory factor to its fragility may be the presence of ancestral 'information' in our subconscious. Ancestral identities may have been evolution's solution to providing individualism, but it could well have led to mental problems which evolution had not encountered in other species.

The spectrum of mental illnesses has long been a reality in humans. I would hope that the linking of additional identities to an ancestral core will come to be seen as a step in the right direction of understanding their involvement in mental health.

The leaders of greater mental awareness have to be the philosophers, psychologists, psychiatrists and mental researchers. No one doubts their objectives will be purely in the interest of the individual and the species. It is their duty and responsibility to educate on matters which will increase mental awareness. **May they unite to make this the century of mental awareness.**

9 781618 976796